Stucky v. Conlee, Parsell, and Nita City

Second Edition

STUCKY V. CONLEE, PARSELL, AND NITA CITY

Second Edition

Gary S. Gildin

Professor of Law
Dickinson Law
Pennsylvania State University

NATIONAL INSTITUTE FOR TRIAL ADVOCACY

Address inquiries to:

Reprint Permission
National Institute for Trial Advocacy
1685 38th Street, Suite 200
Boulder, CO 80301-2735
Phone: (800) 225-6482
Fax: (720) 890-7069
Email: permissions@nita.org

ISBN 978-1-60156-611-9
eISBN 978-1-60156-612-6
FBA 1611

Printed in the United States of America

CONTENTS

ACKNOWLEDGEMENTS vii

CASE SUMMARY 1

INSTRUCTIONS FOR USE AS A FULL TRIAL 3

COMPLAINT 5

ANSWER 9

STIPULATIONS 13

STIPULATED SUMMARY OF MEDICAL EXPENSES 15

DEPOSITIONS 17

    Clayton Stucky 19

    Shelley Elliot 29

    Nelson Digby 33

    Eric Conlee 37

    Lance Parsell 49

    Kurt Lieber 55

EXPERT REPORTS 63

    Report of Plaintiff's Expert Dr. Thomas Goforth 65

    Curriculum Vitae of Dr. Thomas A. Goforth 95

    Report of Defendants' Expert Professor Neil Ellman 97

    Curriculum Vitae of Professor Neil Ellman 101

MEDICAL EXPERT REPORTS 103

    Report of Plaintiff's Medical Expert Dr. Leslie Collins 105

    Curriculum Vitae of Dr. Leslie Collins 111

    Report of Defendants' Medical Expert Dr. Jeremiah Guttman 115

    Curriculum Vitae of Dr. Jeremiah Guttman 119

EXHIBITS 121

    Exhibit 1—Photo of Stucky's vehicle 123

    Exhibit 2—Google Maps diagram map of the East Market Street area. 125

Exhibit 3, 3-A—Google Earth overhead maps of East Market Street area 127

Exhibit 4—Google Earth street view map of railroad tracks on East Market Street 131

Exhibit 5—Street view photo of East Market Street, looking west from where Stucky was stopped 133

Exhibit 6 —Street view of East Market Street where Stucky was stopped. 135

Exhibit 7—Close-up street view of East Market Street where Stucky was stopped 137

Exhibit 8—Photo of door showing address at point of stop. 139

Exhibit 9—Traffic Citation 141

Exhibit 10—Transcript of Preliminary Hearing. 143

Exhibit 11—Bill from Attorney Clinton T. Manges. 173

Exhibit 12—Note from Dr. Stovall excusing Stucky from work. 175

Exhibit 13—Note from Dr. Collins excusing Stucky from work 177

Exhibit 14—Note from Dr. Collins releasing Stucky for work. 179

Exhibit 15—Excerpts from Shelley Elliot's Facebook page. 181

Exhibit 16—Nita City Police Department Traffic Enforcement Training Manual 187

Exhibit 17—Conlee Performance Evaluations from NITA Township for the category "Lack of Prejudice". 199

Exhibit 18—Text message from Lance Parsell to Officer Paget, August 5, YR-2. 229

Exhibit 19—Text message from Officer Paget to Lance Parsell, August 5, YR-2. 231

Exhibit 20—Excerpts from Nita City Police Department Rules, Polices, and Procedures Manual 233

Exhibit 21—Nita City Police Department Traffic Study 245

Exhibit 22—Article from *Nita Gazette*, May 4, YR-1 267

Exhibit 23—TruWeather Report. 269

FINAL JURY INSTRUCTIONS **271**

FINAL VERDICT FORM **275**

Acknowledgements

NITA would like to thank Facebook for permission to use likenesses of its website in this case file. NITA would also like to thank Google for permission to use photos and diagrams from its website in this case file.

CASE SUMMARY

This is a civil rights action for damages arising from alleged racial profiling that resulted in a traffic stop. Plaintiff Clayton Stucky is an African-American who works as a trooper with the Nita State Police. On August 5, YR-2, Stucky was off duty and was driving his personal car, a YR-5 Lexus, with his girlfriend in the front passenger seat. Stucky was wearing what he termed "urban gear" (baggy sweatpants, a baggy shirt, and a New York Yankees hat flipped backwards).

As Stucky drove down East Market Street, at around 11:50 a.m., a marked Nita City Police car pulled him over. Nita City Police Officer Eric Conlee was driving, and Officer Lance Parsell rode in the front passenger seat of the patrol car. Both officers are Caucasian. Conlee and Parsell allege that Stucky was driving over fifty miles per hour in a twenty-five miles per hour zone. In the course of the traffic stop, Conlee asked Stucky for permission to search the trunk of Stucky's car. Stucky refused to consent.

Conlee and Parsell issued Stucky a citation for driving at an unsafe speed. Following a hearing, the district justice found Stucky not guilty of the charged traffic offense. Stucky asserts that he was driving at the speed limit and alleges that Conlee and Stucky pulled him over for "driving while black."

This case file is adaptable for programs and trial advocacy courses of varying degrees of difficulty. In its simplest form, the case file can be used for a trial only against Nita Police Officer Eric Conlee for violation of Plaintiff Clayton Stucky's right to be free from an unreasonable seizure and his right to the equal protection of the laws. To demand a modestly more sophisticated legal and factual theory of the case, the case file can be used for a trial against both Officer Conlee and Officer Lance Parsell.

The case file may also serve as a broader challenge to the policies of the Nita City Police Department by identifying Nita City as the defendant. Stucky alleges that Nita City Police Chief Kurt Lieber was deliberately indifferent with respect to the training and supervision of Conlee and Parsell as to the risk of racial profiling, and that Lieber's indifference was a cause of Conlee's and Parsell's stop of Stucky without probable cause and based upon Stucky's race. This iteration of the case provides the added issue of calling Officers Conlee and Parsell not as defendants but as potentially hostile witnesses.

In its most complex iteration, the case file may be used for a trial against all defendants—Nita City, Officer Conlee, and Officer Parsell. This challenges the advocates to develop a unifying legal and factual theory that accounts for the culpability—or lack of culpability—of multiple defendants.

Finally, in addition to the choice of defendants, the complexity of the trial may be enhanced or reduced by the choice of whether to bifurcate the trial between liability and damages.

The applicable law is contained in the proposed jury instructions set forth at the end of the file. Electronic copies of all exhibits can be found at the following website:

http://bit.ly/1P20Jea
Password: Stucky2

Instructions For Use
As A Full Trial

1. All witnesses can be played by any gender.

2. All witnesses called to testify who have identified the parties, other individuals, or tangible evidence in statements or prior deposition testimony must, if asked, identify the same at trial. Additionally, witnesses have knowledge of all documents on which their signatures appear.

3. Each witness who testified previously agreed under oath at the outset of his or her testimony to give a full and complete description of all material events that occurred and to correct the transcript of such testimony for inaccuracies and completeness before signing the deposition transcript.

4. All exhibits in the case file are authentic. In addition, each exhibit contained in the file is the original of that document unless otherwise noted on the exhibit or as established by the evidence.

5. All signatures are authentic. No advocate may attempt to impeach a witness by arguing that a signature on a transcript, statement, or exhibit does not comport with a signature or initials on an exhibit.

6. Other than what is supplied in the problem itself, there is nothing exceptional or unusual about the background information of any of the witnesses that would bolster or detract from their credibility.

7. The case file is a "closed universe" of facts, and advocates may use only the materials in the file except where the file states otherwise.

8. The Case Summary shall not be used as evidence or for examination or cross-examination of any witness.

Procedural Matters

9. Federal Rules of Evidence and Federal Rules of Civil Procedure apply.

10. The issue of damages, if any, may or may not be addressed in this action. At the outset of the trial, the judge will inform jurors whether the jury will decide what damages, if any, are to be rewarded.

OTHER INSTRUCTIONS

11.   All years in these materials are stated in the following form:

    a.   YR-0 indicates the actual year in which the case is being tried (i.e., the present year);

    b.   YR-1 indicates the next preceding year (please use the actual year);

    c.   YR-2 indicates the second preceding year (please use the actual year), etc.

12.   The applicable law is contained in the case stipulations and proposed jury instructions set forth at the end of this case file.

13.   Electronic copies of all exhibits can be found at the following website:

http://bit.ly/1P20Jea
Password: Stucky2

UNITED STATES DISTRICT COURT
MIDDLE DISTRICT OF NITA

Clayton Stucky,	)	
	)	
Plaintiff,	)	
	)	
v.	)	Civil Action No. CV-7620
	)	
Eric Conlee and Lance Parsell,	)	
in their individual capacities,	)	JURY TRIAL DEMANDED
and Nita City, Nita,	)	
	)	
Defendants.	)	

COMPLAINT

Preliminary Statement

1. Plaintiff Clayton Stucky ("Stucky") brings this action to recover damages for the deprivation of his constitutional rights caused by racial profiling. Two Nita City Police Officers, Eric Conlee ("Conlee") and Lance Parsell ("Parsell") stopped Stucky as Stucky was driving with his girlfriend in Stucky's personal car. Conlee and Parsell lacked any reasonable suspicion or probable cause that justified the stop. Instead, they seized Stucky because he is African-American. Unbeknownst to Conlee and Parsell at the time they stopped Stucky, Stucky is a trooper with the Nita State Police.

   Kurt Lieber ("Lieber") is the Chief of Police of Nita City. As such, he is responsible for supervising and training police officers in Nita City, including Conlee and Parsell. Lieber was deliberately indifferent with respect to his supervision and training of Conlee and Parsell as to the risk of racial profiling. Lieber also acquiesced in and ratified the actions of Conlee and Parsell when they stopped Stucky based upon his race.

   Lieber has final authority in Nita City to establish the policies, rules, and procedures of Nita City Police Department. Lieber also has final authority for the supervision and training of police officers in Nita City in the Nita Police Department. Therefore Lieber's action and inaction in this case represent the policy of Nita City and subject the City to liability under 42 U.S.C. § 1983.

Statement of Jurisdiction

2. Stucky brings this action under 42 U.S.C. § 1983, which provides a civil action against persons who, under color of law, deprive a citizen of federal constitutional rights. This Court has jurisdiction over all Counts in this matter pursuant to 28 U.S. C. §§ 1331 and 1343(3).

COUNT I: UNREASONABLE SEIZURE

(Stucky v. Conlee and Parsell)

The Parties

3. Plaintiff Stucky has been employed by the Nita State Police as a trooper since January of YR-12.

4. On August 5, YR-2, Defendant Conlee was employed as a police officer by the Nita City Police Department.

5. At all times material to the events that gave rise to this Complaint, Conlee was acting under color of law within the meaning of 42 U.S.C. § 1983.

6. Conlee is sued in his individual capacity.

7. On August 5, YR-2, Defendant Parsell was employed as a police officer by the Nita City Police Department.

8. At all times material to the events that gave rise to this Complaint, Parsell was acting under color of law within the meaning of 42 U.S.C. § 1983.

9. Parsell is sued in his individual capacity.

Conlee's and Parsell's Stop of Stucky

10. On August 5, YR-2 at around 11:50 a.m., Stucky was driving his personal car on East Market Street in Nita.

11. Stucky was not wearing his Nita State Police uniform.

12. Stucky's girlfriend was in the car with Stucky.

13. At the same time, Conlee and Parsell were in uniform and were driving on East Market Street in a marked Nita City Police Department car that displayed a standard red and blue bar light.

14. Conlee and Parsell did not have a basic calibrated stopwatch, an ESP traffic control device, Accutrack, VASCAR, or any other calibrated speed timing device in their car.

15. Conlee and Parsell did not have a calibrated speedometer in the car.

16. Conlee and Parsell activated all the emergency lights on their car and stopped Stucky's car.

17. Conlee and Parsell's stopping of Stucky's car was a seizure within the meaning of the Fourth and Fourteenth Amendments to the United States Constitution.

18. Conlee and Parsell did not have reasonable suspicion or probable cause to stop Stucky's car.

19. Conlee and Parsell issued a citation to Stucky for driving at a speed that was not reasonable or prudent for the conditions.

20. On November 7, YR-2, Municipal Court Judge Helen L. Daley found Stucky not guilty on the charge of driving at a speed that was not reasonable or prudent under the conditions.

21. Conlee's and Parsell's stopping of Stucky's car without probable cause or reasonable suspicion caused damages to Stucky.

22. Conlee's and Parsell acted in reckless disregard of Stucky's Fourth and Fourteenth Amendment rights.

COUNT II: DEPRIVATION OF EQUAL PROTECTION

(Stucky v. Conlee and Parsell)

23. Stucky incorporates by reference paragraphs 3 through 22.

24. As an African-American person, Stucky is a member of a protected class.

25. Conlee and Parsell purposefully stopped Stucky because Stucky is African-American.

26. By purposefully stopping Stucky because of Stucky's race, Conlee and Parsell deprived Stucky of the equal protection of the law within the meaning of the Fourteenth Amendment to the United States Constitution.

27. By purposefully stopping Stucky because of Stucky's race, Conlee and Parsell caused damages to Stucky.

28. Conlee and Parsell acted in reckless disregard of Stucky's Fourteenth Amendment rights.

COUNT III: MUNICIPAL LIABILITY FOR UNREASONABLE SEIZURE AND DEPRIVATION OF EQUAL PROTECTION

(Stucky v. Nita City)

29. Stucky incorporates by reference paragraphs 3 through 28.

30. On August 5, YR-2, Defendant Lieber was employed as Chief of Police by the Nita City Police Department.

31. At all times material to the events that gave rise to this Complaint, Lieber was acting under color of law within the meaning of 42 U.S.C. § 1983.

32. Lieber's duties as Chief of Police included training and supervision of Nita City police officers. Lieber's duties as Chief of Police included training and supervision of Conlee and Parsell.

33. Lieber was deliberately indifferent with respect to his supervision of Conlee and Parsell as to the risk of racial profiling.

34. Lieber was deliberately indifferent with respect to his training of Conlee and Parsell as to the risk of racial profiling

35. Lieber also acquiesced in and ratified the actions of Conlee and Parsell in stopping Stucky without probable cause or reasonable suspicion and based upon his race.

36. Lieber's action was a cause of Conlee's and Parsell's stop of Stucky without probable cause or reasonable suspicion and based upon Stucky's race.

37. Lieber possesses final authority in Nita City to establish the policies, rules, and procedures of the Nita City Police Department.

38. Lieber also possesses final authority in Nita City for the supervision and training of police officers in the Nita City Police Department.

39. Lieber's action and inaction in this case represents the policy of Nita City and subjects the City to liability under 42 U.S.C. § 1983.

Demand for Judgment

40. Stucky requests the following relief:

    A. Compensatory damages from all defendants for humiliation, pain and suffering, emotional distress, mental anguish, and/or related emotional damages that Stucky has incurred or will incur in the future as a result of the August 5, YR-2, incident.

    B. Compensatory damages from all defendants for lost wages, legal bills, medical bills, and/or other expenses that Stucky has incurred or will incur in the future as a result of the August 5, YR-2, incident.

    C. Compensatory damages from all defendants for the value of the federal constitutional rights invaded to Stucky.

    D. Punitive damages from defendants Conlee and Parsell.

    E. Reasonable attorneys' fees from all defendants pursuant to 42 U.S.C. § 1988.

    F. Such other and further relief that the Court may deem just.

Respectfully submitted,

/s/Sharon K. Coby
Sharon K. Coby
ACLU of Nita
105 North Front Street, Suite 225
Nita City, Nita 09101
Phone: 322-555-6827
FAX: 322-555-6895
Email:Scoby@aclunita.nita

UNITED STATES DISTRICT COURT
MIDDLE DISTRICT OF NITA

Clayton Stucky,   )
)
        Plaintiff,   )
)
    v.   )   Civil Action No. CV-7620
)
Eric Conlee et al.,   )
)   JURY TRIAL DEMANDED
        Defendants.   )

ANSWER

Defendants Eric Conlee, Lance Parsell, and Nita City, by their attorney David Payton, answer the Complaint as follows:

1. Defendants admit that Eric Conlee and Lance Parsell are Nita City Police Officers. Defendants admit that Conlee and Parsell stopped Stucky as Stucky was driving with his girlfriend in Stucky's personal car, but deny any implication that they were aware of these facts when they stopped Stucky. Defendants admit that Conlee and Parsell were unaware that Stucky was a trooper with the Nita State Police when they decided to stop Stucky. Defendants deny all remaining allegations of the first paragraph of the Preliminary Statement.

   Defendants admit that Kurt Lieber is the Chief of Police of Nita City and is responsible for supervising and training police officers in Nita City, including Conlee and Parsell. Defendants deny the remaining allegations of the second paragraph of the Preliminary Statement.

   The third paragraph of the Preliminary Statement is a legal conclusion to which no response is required under the applicable Federal Rules of Civil Procedure. Alternatively, defendants deny the allegations of the third paragraph of the Preliminary Statement.

   Defendants specifically deny that they violated Stucky's constitutional rights or otherwise engaged in racial profiling in stopping Stucky's car, which was being driven at an unsafe speed at the time of the stop. By way of further answer, the policies of the Nita City Police Department and Nita City are to treat all persons equally, regardless of their race, sex, nationality, or religion.

2. Defendants admit the allegations of paragraph 2.

3. After reasonable investigation, defendants are without knowledge or information sufficient to form a belief as to the truth of the averments contained in paragraph 3.

4. Defendants admit the allegations of paragraph 4.

5. Defendants admit the allegations of paragraph 5.

6. Defendants admit the allegations of paragraph 6.

7. Defendants admit the allegations of paragraph 7.

8. Defendants admit the allegations of paragraph 8.

9. Defendants admit the allegations of paragraph 9.

10. Defendants admit the allegations of paragraph 10, but deny any implication that they were aware of these facts when they stopped Stucky.

11. Defendants admit the allegations of paragraph 11.

12. Defendants admit the allegation of paragraph 12, but deny any implication that they were aware of this fact when they stopped Stucky.

13. Defendants admit the allegations of paragraph 13.

14. Defendants admit the allegations of paragraph 14, but deny any implication that they were not empowered to stop a car for driving at an unsafe speed.

15. Defendants admit the allegations of paragraph 15, but deny any implication that they were not empowered to stop a car for driving at an unsafe speed.

16. Defendants admit the allegations of paragraph 16.

17. Defendants admit the allegations of paragraph 17.

18. Defendants deny the allegations of paragraph 18.

19. Defendants admit the allegations of paragraph 19.

20. Defendants admit the allegations of paragraph 20, but deny any implication that they did not have reasonable suspicion or probable cause to stop Stucky for driving at a speed that was not reasonable or prudent under the circumstances.

21. Defendants deny the allegations of paragraph 21.

22. Defendants deny the allegations of paragraph 22.

23. Defendants incorporate by reference their answers to paragraphs 3 through 22.

24. Defendants admit the allegations of paragraph 24.

25. Defendants deny the allegations of paragraph 25. Defendants were not aware of Stucky's race when they made the decision to stop him for driving at a speed that was not reasonable or prudent under the circumstances.

26. Defendants deny the allegations of paragraph 26.

27. Defendants deny the allegations of paragraph 27.

28. Defendants deny the allegations of paragraph 28.

29. Defendants incorporate by reference their answers to paragraphs 3 through 28.

30. Defendants admit the allegations of paragraph 30.

31. Defendants admit the allegations of paragraph 31.

32. Defendants admit the allegations of paragraph 32.

33. Defendants deny the allegations of paragraph 33. To the contrary, the policies of the Nita City Police Department are to treat all persons equally regardless of their race, sex, nationality, or religion.

34. Defendants deny the allegations of paragraph 34. To the contrary, the policies of the Nita City Police Department are to treat all persons equally regardless of their race, sex, nationality, or religion.

35. Defendants deny the allegations of paragraph 35. By way of further answer, Conlee and Parsell had probable cause and reasonable suspicion to stop Stucky.

36. Defendants deny the allegations of paragraph 36. By way of further answer, Conlee and Parsell had probable cause and reasonable suspicion to stop Stucky.

37. The allegations of paragraph 37 are a legal conclusion to which no response is required under the applicable Federal Rules of Civil Procedure. Alternatively, defendants deny the allegations of paragraph 37. By way of further answer, the policies of the Nita City Police Department and Nita City are to treat all persons equally, regardless of their race, sex, nationality, or religion.

38. The allegations of paragraph 38 are a legal conclusion to which no response is required under the applicable Federal Rules of Civil Procedure. Alternatively, defendants deny the allegations of paragraph 38. By way of further answer, the policies of the Nita City Police Department and Nita City are to treat all persons equally, regardless of their race, sex, nationality, or religion.

39. The allegations of paragraph 39 are a legal conclusion to which no response is required under the applicable Federal Rules of Civil Procedure. Alternatively, defendants deny the allegations of paragraph 39. By way of further answer, the policies of the Nita City Police Department and Nita City are to treat all persons equally, regardless of their race, sex, nationality, or religion. Defendants specifically deny that their actions and/or policies are in violation of the Constitution or that Chief Lieber's actions or inactions subject Nita City to liability.

40. Defendants admit that paragraph 40 sets forth the relief that Stucky is requesting, but denies that they are liable for any of the relief sought in paragraph 40.

41. Defendants deny all remaining allegations not specifically admitted.

FIRST AFFIRMATIVE DEFENSE

42. The Complaint fails to state a claim upon which relief may be granted.

SECOND AFFIRMATIVE DEFENSE

43. Defendants Conlee and Parsell are entitled to qualified immunity.

WHEREFORE, Defendants Eric Conlee, Lance Parsell, and Nita City respectfully request that the Complaint be dismissed and that judgment be entered in their favor.

Respectfully submitted,

/s/ David Payton
David Payton
Payton and Payton
P.O. Box 1976
3513 North Front Street
Nita City, Nita 09102
Phone: 322-555-0485
FAX: 322-555-5238

Clayton Stucky,

    Plaintiff,

v.

Eric Conlee et al.,

    Defendants.

)
)
)
)
)
)
)
)
)
)
)

Civil Action No. CV-7620

JURY TRIAL DEMANDED

STIPULATIONS

1. The race of the witnesses is as follows: Nelson Digby, Eric Conlee, Lance Parsell, Kurt Lieber, and Professor Neil Ellman are all Caucasian. Clayton Stucky and Thomas Goforth are African-American. Shelley Elliot's father is Caucasian and her mother is Hispanic; Shelley has a light complexion.

2. Nita City had a population of 45,817 in the YR-3 census.

3. Market Street, where the traffic stop occurred, is ten miles away from the Nita County Airport.

4. Section 3362 of the Nita Motor Vehicle Code provides, in pertinent part, as follows:

    a) Any person who drives a vehicle in excess of the maximum lawful speed limit is guilty of a summary offense and shall, upon conviction, be sentenced to pay a fine as follows:

        i. $42.50 for violating a maximum speed of sixty-five miles per hour;

        ii. $35 for violating any other maximum speed limit.

    b) Any person exceeding the maximum speed limit by more than five miles per hour shall pay an additional fine of $2 per mile for each mile in excess of five miles per hour over the maximum speed limit.

    c) The rate of speed of any vehicle may be timed on a highway by a police officer using a motor vehicle equipped with a speedometer that has been tested for accuracy within a period of sixty days prior to the alleged violation. In ascertaining the speed of a vehicle by use of a speedometer, the speed shall be timed for a distance of not less than three-tenths of a mile.

    d) The rate of speed of any vehicle may be timed on any highway by a police officer using a mechanical or electrical speed timing device. No person may be convicted upon evidence obtained through the use of a mechanical or electrical speed timing device in an area where the legal speed limit is less than fifty-five miles per hour if the speed recorded is less than ten miles per hour in excess of the legal speed limit. No person may be convicted

ce obtained through the use of a mechanical or electrical speed timing device
here the legal speed limit is greater than or equal to fifty-five miles per hour
recorded is less than seven miles per hour in excess of the legal speed limit.

the Nita Motor Vehicle Code provides, in pertinent part, as follows:

ıall drive a vehicle at a speed greater than is reasonable and prudent under
the conditions and having regard to the actual and potential hazards then existing, nor at
a speed greater than will permit the driver to bring his vehicle to a stop within the assured
clear distance ahead. Consistent with the foregoing, every person shall drive at a safe and
appropriate speed when approaching and crossing an intersection or railroad grade crossing, when approaching and going around a curve, when approaching a hill crest, when
traveling upon any narrow and winding roadway and when special hazards exist with
respect to pedestrians or other traffic or by reason of weather or highway conditions.

6. The Nita Supreme Court has ruled that the requirements of Section 3362(c) apply equally to
using a motor vehicle equipped with a speedometer to obtain a valid estimate of speed under
Section 3361.

7. Defendants Conlee and Parsell filed a motion for summary judgment on the ground of
qualified immunity. The district court denied the motion, ruling that the constitutional rights
allegedly violated were clearly established at the time of the traffic stop.

UNITED STATES DISTRICT COURT
MIDDLE DISTRICT OF NITA

Clayton Stucky,	)	
	)	
Plaintiff,	)	Civil Action No. CV-7620
	)	
v.	)	
	)	
Eric Conlee et al.,	)	JURY TRIAL DEMANDED
	)	
Defendants.	)	

STIPULATED SUMMARY OF MEDICAL EXPENSES

Pursuant to Federal Rule of Evidence 1006, the parties stipulate that the following is a true and accurate summary of the medical expenses incurred by Clayton Stucky for treatment by Drs. Anna Stovall and Leslie Collins, including prescription medications, between August YR-2 and November YR-1.

Dr. Stovall:	$500.00
Dr. Collins:	$1,820.00
Prescription Costs:	$4,458.90

Defendants do not stipulate that any of these expenses were caused by the actions of any of the defendants and continue to deny that any defendant violated the constitutional rights of Clayton Stucky.

/s/ *Sharon Coby*
ACLU of Nita
Attorney for Plaintiff

/s/ *David Payton*
Payton and Payton
Attorney for Defendants

DEPOSITIONS

DEPOSITION OF CLAYTON STUCKY

1   My name is Clayton Stucky. I live at 1100 Ambruster Lane in Nita City, Nita. I am thirty-six

2   years old. On August 5, YR-2, I was living with my eight-year-old son, Zachary. I share joint

3   custody of him following my divorce from my first wife. On November 15, YR-1, I married

4   Shelley Elliot, who has two daughters. We all live together now as a family with three kids,

5   even though I haven't officially adopted Shelley's girls.

6

7   I have been a trooper with the Nita State Police since January, YR-12. I was assigned to

8   the Barrington barracks, which is about a one-hour drive from my home in Nita City. My

9   principal duty is traffic enforcement on the Nita Turnpike, including dealing with acci-

10 dents and enforcing traffic speed regulations. Of course, we also deal with any criminal

11 activity—including transport of drugs—that happens along the turnpike. I received my

12 basic training at the Nita State Police Academy, and fulfill my continuing education re-

13 quirements there as well. Basic training includes instruction on cultural sensitivity and

14 the avoidance of racial profiling. I've also attended advanced programs designed to ensure

15 that troopers don't subconsciously use race or ethnicity in our law enforcement decisions.

16

17 Before joining the state police, I left high school at age sixteen and worked in a factory.

18 When I was eighteen, I obtained my GED and enlisted in the Army for four years. After

19 receiving an honorable discharge, I worked for my father in his grocery store for a couple

20 of years. I applied for positions with the Nita City Police and Fire Departments at the same

21 time that I applied for a position with the Nita State Police. I received offers from all three

22 agencies and accepted the position with the State Police.

23

24 The morning of August 5, YR-2, I fed Zachary breakfast, got him dressed, and took him to

25 his mother's house, where he was going to spend the next several days. I was scheduled to

26 begin working at 3:00 p.m. I picked up my then-girlfriend, Shelley, to run a few errands, do

27 some shopping, and have lunch together downtown before I had to leave for work. I wasn't

28 wearing my police uniform, but was dressed in "urban gear"—baggy sweatpants, a baggy

1 shirt, and a New York Yankees hat worn backwards—and sunglasses. I drove my personal

2 car, a YR-5 four-door Lexus. I leased the Lexus as a pre-owned car in YR-3. Exhibit 1 is a

3 true and accurate photo of my car.

4

5 Shelley and I stopped at the dry cleaners to drop off some laundry, browsed at a couple

6 of clothing stores, and around 11:30 got back in the car to go to lunch. I was driving in

7 the right lane on East Market Street in downtown Nita on the way to the restaurant, and

8 Shelley was in the front passenger seat. Both of us were wearing our seat belts.

9

10 East Market Street is one of the main thoroughfares in the city. It's a one-way street with

11 two driving lanes as well as space for parked cars on both sides of the roadway. The

12 roadway was a bit damp, but not saturated with puddles or water. There was a mist in

13 the air, but it wasn't raining. Shelley and I didn't have umbrellas because it wasn't raining

14 when I picked her up.

15

16 Traffic on Market Street was normal. I drove in the right travel lane. I approached a red

17 light in the 400 block of East Market Street, where it intersects with Broad Street, and

18 stopped at the light. I was the first car in the right travel lane at the light. I noticed a marked

19 Nita City police car next to me, which was the first car in the left travel lane, stopped at

20 the light. I looked over and saw two officers sitting in the front seat. Eric Conlee was driv-

21 ing, and Lance Parsell was in the front passenger seat, though I didn't know their names

22 at that time. Both of the officers looked over at me as we sat at the light, and I nodded my

23 head at them.

24

25 When the light turned green, I proceeded down the street at about the speed limit, twenty

26 to twenty-five miles per hour. The Nita City police car was quick off the mark and pulled

27 out ahead of me several car lengths before suddenly slowing down. I didn't think anything

28 about it. They serve warrants and do things of that nature, so I assumed they were out

29 there looking for somebody. Just before crossing the old railroad tracks on East Market

30 Street, I passed the police car on the right as it slowed further. A few seconds later, I saw

1   the red and blue lights of the police car flashing. I thought they had located the individual

2   they were looking for, and when I saw in the rear view mirror that the police car had

3   pulled into the right lane behind me, I thought the officers were trying to pull over to the

4   curb on the right side of the street. I pulled into the left lane to move out of their way.

5   When the police car moved back into the left lane behind me, I realized they wanted me

6   to pull over.

7

8   Exhibits 2 through 4 are screen shots of a map and street view from Google Earth

9   that truly and accurately depict the area of East Market Street where I was driving on

10 August 5, YR-2. The overhead lights of the police car came on as I crossed Fulton Street.

11 I ultimately stopped my car on the left side of East Market between the NV Bar and Grill

12 and Temptations, just beyond Local Way. That neighborhood is well known as an area

13 where drug deals go down. Exhibits 5 through 8 are true and accurate photos of where

14 I stopped my car.

15

16 I pulled my car over to the left parking lane and stopped the car. Shelley asked, "Why are

17 they pulling you over, Clayton?" I said, "I'm not sure. We'll find out in a second." The police

18 car parked at the curb behind my car, and both officers got out. Officer Parsell stood back

19 toward the right rear of my car. Officer Conlee came up to the driver's window and in an

20 agitated tone said, "Let me see your license and registration." I calmly and politely asked,

21 "What did you pull me over for?" Conlee became even more upset, started jabbing his

22 finger at me, and said, "I am not going to tell you again. Let me see your license and regis-

23 tration." When he shouted that, Shelley became very upset and began to cry. She sobbed,

24 "Why is he yelling at you?" At that moment, my attention turned to Shelley and I said,

25 "Calm down, calm down, everything is going to be fine."

26

27 I reached over to the glove box of my car to get the registration, looked back towards

28 Conlee, and calmly asked, "Can you please tell me why you pulled me over?" At that point,

29 he lowered his head to the window and screamed, "Just shut up and give me your license

30 and registration." That's when Parsell came over and stood at the window next to Officer

1 Conlee. He laid his right hand on the butt of his gun, and took a defensive stance, ready to

2 pull the gun. I recognized that stance from my own experience as a trooper.

3

4 Up until that moment, I hadn't really considered my situation, but as soon as I saw his

5 hand on the gun, I got scared. Shocked and scared. Suddenly I wasn't just an off-duty

6 state trooper getting routinely pulled over. In that moment, I realized that I was one more

7 anonymous black man about to get into a confrontation with the police.

8

9 When you are African-American, you are well aware that every encounter with white po-

10 lice officers is potentially fraught with danger. A whole series of names flashed through

11 my mind. Eric Garner, who was put in an illegal chokehold and killed by a white police of-

12 ficer for selling cigarettes, and Michael Brown, an unarmed black eighteen-year-old shot

13 and killed in Ferguson by officer Darren Wilson. When you're black, the most routine traf-

14 fic stop can be fatal. Walter Scott was killed while running away from a police officer who

15 had made a daytime traffic stop for a non-functioning brake light. Philando Castile was

16 pulled over for a broken taillight and then shot and killed in front of his girlfriend and her

17 four-year-old daughter as he sat in the driver's seat—I mean, the officer shot him with a

18 little girl in the car, just because he was reaching for his license.

19

20 I'm not embarrassed to admit how scared I was. I knew the situation here was totally

21 wrong, a bad, bad scenario, so I wanted someone else to hear what was going on. I'd

22 dropped my cell phone a couple days earlier, and the camera wasn't working, so I knew

23 I couldn't record the stop. It didn't even occur to me to ask Shelley to start recording—

24 she was crying so hard that I couldn't really talk to her. I picked up my cell phone and

25 called my station commander, Sergeant Digby. I told him I had been pulled over by two

26 Nita City police officers and didn't know why they stopped me or were yelling at me.

27 I didn't specifically tell the sergeant at that time that I was concerned for my safety.

28 Sergeant Digby told me to just hang up the phone, cooperate with the officers, and that

29 he would call the Nita City police chief to report the incident. Digby told me to call him

30 back once the encounter ended.

1 My making that call really seemed to anger Conlee. He told me to, "Get off the fucking

2 phone." Conlee then asked me if he could look to see what was in a black bag that was

3 sitting in the back seat of the car. In my mind, this confirmed my suspicion that they had

4 profiled me as a drug dealer based on my race, dress, and the fact that I was driving a

5 Lexus. But in my training as a police officer, I knew that cooperating with an aggressor can

6 help calm an incident. In order to try to settle him down, I agreed. I started to reach back

7 for the bag, but saw Parsell's grip tighten on his gun. I remembered Levar Jones getting

8 shot just for reaching back into his car for the ID the officer requested, and I returned my

9 hands to the steering wheel. By that time I'd broken into a cold sweat and was shaking.

10 I told Conlee that he could get the bag out of the back seat. Conlee reached in through the

11 back window and opened the bag, which contained my 35mm Nikon camera. Conlee then

12 asked to see the backpack that also was in the back seat. I said yes, but before consenting

13 I specifically told him that this was the last item that I would allow him to search. After

14 Conlee opened the backpack and found it contained only a book and my checkbook, Con-

15 lee asked me to pop the trunk of the car. I told him that, as I had just stated, I would not

16 consent to any further searches. It was clear that Conlee was not going to stop searching,

17 and I was not about to continue allowing him to violate my constitutional rights.

18

19 I handed Conlee my driver's license and registration. I had my state police badge and ID

20 card in a separate badge case in my pocket. I didn't show the badge or ID to either officer,

21 nor did I tell them that I was a police officer, because state police aren't allowed to use our

22 office to obtain special treatment.

23

24 Conlee went back to his police car. Parsell remained at the window of my car. Parsell

25 looked very uncomfortable and sheepish, as if he knew that what was going on wasn't

26 right. Parsell never said a word to me. While Parsell kept his right hand on his gun, at no

27 time did Officers Parsell or Conlee take their weapons out of their holsters.

28

29 After about ten minutes, Conlee came back to my car, told me that I had been driving

30 fifty-five miles per hour, which was way too fast for the weather conditions, and handed

1   me a citation. I said, "Are you kidding, there is no way I was driving anywhere near that

2   fast. And what weather conditions are you talking about?" Conlee ignored my question

3   and asked me to sign the citation to acknowledge that I had received it. Exhibit 9 is a true

4   and accurate copy of the citation. I know that a motorist is under no legal obligation to

5   sign a citation, so I refused to sign. Conlee then said, "I understand that you're a state

6   trooper." I said, "Yes." Conlee then pointed his finger at me and screamed, "You better be

7   careful who you say you are. Thirty years I've been on the job, and I've never been disre-

8   spected by another police officer like you." I wasn't even sure what that was supposed to

9   mean, since I'd been polite and cooperative throughout the encounter, but I knew better

10   than to escalate the situation. I asked if he was done. Conlee said, "Yes," and I drove away.

11   I never told Conlee that "I know the drill." I never asked Conlee to "extend a courtesy to

12   a brother" or any words to that effect.

13

14   I pulled over after a few blocks and called Sergeant Digby to let him know what had hap-

15   pened since my first call. I was shaking so badly that it was hard to use the phone—I don't

16   know if I was angry or if it was just the adrenaline from how scared I'd been. I said, "Sarge,

17   they used my race. They pulled me over because, you know, I'm driving this car and I'm

18   black. There was no other reason they pulled me over. I wasn't doing anything." He told

19   me that he had called Nita City Police Chief Lieber to let him know about the stop. Lieber

20   promised Digby he would call in Conlee and Parsell to ask them about the stop.

21

22   After reading Conlee's deposition transcript, I was even more certain that I was a victim

23   of racial profiling. Clearly he saw me as his meal ticket to getting back to being a street

24   cop rather than standing around a courtroom or driving prisoners to and from court. No

25   doubt Conlee thought Chief Lieber would conclude Conlee was being underutilized if he

26   scored a drug bust.

27

28   As state troopers, we could be disciplined if we violate the Motor Vehicle Code or if we act

29   in a way unbecoming a police officer, even if the conduct happens while we are off-duty.

30   I have never been stopped or received a traffic citation since I joined the state police.

1   In April of YR-3, a person who I stopped accused me of seizing and keeping drugs from his

2   car. A grand jury was empaneled to investigate, and the state police conducted an internal

3   investigation. The grand jury didn't issue an indictment, and the internal investigation in

4   January of YR-2 found the charges to be unfounded. There is no denying that was an in-

5   credibly stressful experience—how do you defend yourself against something that never

6   happened? And here I was, nine months after being cleared, once again having to defend

7   a false accusation of wrongdoing.

8

9   I hired an attorney to represent me before the district justice on the traffic citation.

10   Following a hearing, the district justice found me not guilty. Exhibit 10 is a true and ac-

11   curate copy of the transcript of that hearing. Exhibit 11 is a true and accurate copy of

12   the bill from my attorney.

13

14   I was extremely upset about the fact that I had been stopped because of my race. In a pe-

15   culiar way, the fact that I issue traffic tickets as part of my job as an officer with the Nita

16   State Police made my reaction stronger. I certainly was not fazed by being pulled over, not

17   at the beginning of the traffic stop. I was completely relaxed—until Conlee started scream-

18   ing at me and Parsell put his hand on his gun. All the horrible things that have happened to

19   unarmed black people changed from something that made me angry into something that

20   made me afraid for my life. And I was painfully aware that there was no possible reason

21   Conlee and Parsell pulled me over other than the fact I'm black and driving a nice car. This

22   was a classic instance of being stopped for "driving while black." It's hard for me to put in

23   words what it feels like to be treated as less than a whole person solely because of the color

24   of your skin, no matter how hard you work and what you accomplish in your life. I couldn't

25   stop thinking about the stop and kept trying to make sense of what the officers did. And

26   if this could happen to me as a trooper, what hope is there that my son, Zachary, can ever

27   go through life without being a victim of discrimination? I mean, I've had the training.

28   I know what threats the police are watching for, and I still almost whipped around to grab

29   something off the back seat! It's natural to suppose you're being regarded as just a normal

30   human being, just obeying a request. How close had I come to getting shot?

1 That was a thought I couldn't get out of my mind. I began getting migraine headaches. I'd

2 get nauseated, and it felt like the side of my head was going to bust open. I would wake

3 up in the middle of the night, sweating and shaking, and my head would just be pound-

4 ing. I couldn't eat, either—I lost ten pounds because my stomach always felt knotted up.

5 The headaches just kept coming, more and more often. I tried to tough it out, but Shelley

6 could see that I was really suffering. At her urging, I finally went to see my family doctor,

7 Dr. Stovall, in December of YR-2. After examining me, Dr. Stovall sent a note to my police

8 department requesting medical leave for one month. Exhibit 12 is a true and accurate

9 copy of that note. I saw Dr. Stovall a couple more times during that month, and though she

10 tried to work with me to get the pain and the nausea under control, she eventually told

11 me that the headaches were from issues that she couldn't deal with as a family doctor. At

12 that point, she referred me to Dr. Collins.

13

14 I first met with Dr. Collins in March of YR-1. Over the course of the next seven months,

15 Dr. Collins saw me around twenty times. My treatment ended in November of YR-1.

16 Dr. Collins really understood what I was going through. She gave me audiotapes of

17 guided meditations designed to relieve stress, and taught me some breathing and other

18 exercises to help me try to relax. In addition, she prescribed Imitrex for the migraine

19 headaches and another drug to help me sleep better.

20

21 Besides impacting my health, this stress has seriously impacted my career. I had trouble

22 concentrating at work. Corporals began turning back my reports because I didn't sign my

23 name, or I would leave out vital information that we needed. I'd be sitting in my police

24 vehicle sometimes, just doing nothing. The corporal would drive up on me just to make

25 sure I was OK, and he'd see me just sitting there. My senior officers told me that they

26 felt I was just not there mentally. Sergeant Digby suggested that I go to the Members As-

27 sistance Program, but I felt too embarrassed to do so. State troopers are supposed to be

28 tough, to be able to handle stressful situations, and here I was falling apart over a traffic

29 stop. I guess I thought someone would laugh at me—anyway, I didn't take advantage of

30 the Members Assistance Program.

1   Dr. Collins issued a note to the state police asking that I be excused from work for medical

2   reasons. Exhibit 13 is that note and Exhibit 14 is the note clearing me to return to work.

3   I took sick leave for a month in March and again in July of YR-1, and several other days

4   here and there totaling another month. That sick leave had a serious financial impact for

5   me. I don't have it to use if Shelley or Zachary or the girls get sick, so my financial cushion

6   for a family emergency is gone. And if all of us stayed healthy, I could have cashed in that

7   accumulated sick leave at the end of my career. I also was not able to take the test for

8   promotion from trooper to corporal, which was given in March of YR-1. My state police

9   salary in YR-2 was a little over $56,000 per year. The promotion would have resulted in

10 an increase in salary of $8,000 per year. The exam is offered only every four years, so now

11 I can't take the exam and seek promotion until March of YR+3.

I have read this deposition, and the answers are true to the best of my knowledge and
belief.

/s/Clayton Stucky
Clayton Stucky
Date: January 4, YR-0

/s/Leslie Poolman
Leslie Poolman
Notary Public

DEPOSITION OF SHELLEY ELLIOT

1   My name is Shelley Elliot. I am thirty-three years old. I am Hispanic. On August 5, YR-2,

2   I was divorced and living in Nita City, Nita with my two daughters and my mother. I had

3   been dating Clayton Stucky for two years at that time, and we married in November of

4   YR-1. We live at 110 Ambruster Lane in Nita City, Nita, with my daughters and, the weeks

5   when Clayton has custody, his son, Zachary.

6

7   I work at the Guardado Transition Center. We help Hispanics in the Nita community fur-

8   ther their English language skills. I've been with the Center for four years. I also volun-

9   teer at an organization that advocates for Latino persons. Before I began working at the

10 Center, I was intake assistant to the Nita City Human Relations Commission. I was the

11 initial contact for people complaining of racial discrimination in employment, housing,

12 or public accommodations. I filled out the intake forms with the information that they

13 gave me, so I've heard a lot of really appalling stories about discrimination over the years.

14

15 On August 5, YR-2, Clayton picked me up in his car at my mother's house around 10:00 a.m.

16 I had taken the day off from work so that we could do some shopping and have lunch

17 together. Clayton usually works the 3:00 p.m. to midnight shift and has to take care of his

18 son on the weekends, so it's hard for us to spend time alone unless I take an occasional

19 day off during the week. That day we stopped at a couple of boutique clothing stores in

20 downtown Nita, and then it was time to head for lunch.

21

22 We were on East Market Street heading for the restaurant when I noticed Clayton look-

23 ing intently in the rear-view mirror. He moved over to the left-hand lane, and then pulled

24 over to the curb on the left. I looked out the back window and saw a police car with its

25 overhead lights flashing. My initial thought was that these were some police friends of

26 Clayton who just wanted to say hello. When I asked Clayton why he was pulled over,

27 however, he looked concerned and answered that he had no idea.

1   Two officers got out of the police car. The larger one—who I now know is Conlee—came

2   up to the window next to Clayton. I could tell from the look in Conlee's eye and his swag-

3   ger that something bad was going down. Even before he spoke, I could tell that he was

4   angry. In a snarky tone, Conlee barked, "Give me your license and registration!" Somehow

5   Clayton stayed calm—no doubt because of his training as a police officer—and asked

6   why Conlee had pulled him over. This really set Conlee off. He pointed his finger at Clay-

7   ton and started screaming that he was not going to say it again, and that if he knew what

8   was good for him, Clayton should shut up and hand over the license and registration.

9   His attitude shocked and frightened me. I started crying, and Clayton reached over, took

10   my hand, and told me not to worry, that everything would be fine. I still can't believe he

11   stayed so calm.

12

13   As Clayton fetched the registration papers from the glove box, he again asked Conlee po-

14   litely why he had been pulled over. Conlee stuck his head in Clayton's face and shouted,

15   "Shut up, give me the license and registration." Conlee was being so hostile that the younger

16   officer, Parsell, came up to the window as well. My fear went through the roof when I saw

17   that his hand was on his gun. All I could think about was Diamond Reynolds, sitting in the

18   passenger seat while a cop shot her boyfriend, Philando Castile, four times. Here I was, in

19   the passenger seat of my boyfriend's car while a cop stood there with his hand on his gun.

20   All I could think was, "It can't happen again, can it? Please, God, don't let it happen again."

21

22   After Parsell came up by the window, Clayton took out his cell phone and made a call.

23   Despite Clayton's efforts to calm me, by this point I was so hysterical that I didn't hear

24   what he said on the phone. But it really set Conlee off. He told Clayton to, "Get off the

25   fucking phone." Clayton hung up, then Conlee asked to see what was in two bags that

26   were in the back seat. I remember some argument between Clayton and Conlee about

27   searching the trunk, but I can't remember exactly what was said.

28

29   Conlee went back to the police car and Parsell stood guard at the window. I could tell from

30   his body language and the fact that he didn't say a word that Parsell knew that Conlee had

1 crossed the line, but felt helpless to do anything about it. Still, he didn't take his hand off

2 that gun. I sat there, frozen, not wanting to do anything that might cause him to draw it.

3 I barely breathed.

4

5 After a while, Conlee came back to the car and handed Clayton a speeding ticket. Conlee

6 said that he was driving fifty-five miles an hour on a wet roadway. That was preposterous.

7 We were just enjoying a leisurely day together, and there's no way anyone could or would

8 be driving that fast through downtown on Market Street in the middle of the day. Besides,

9 it wasn't even raining. At most there was some mist in the air. I started crying again, but

10 more from anger than from fear. There was no legitimate reason for Conlee's actions. In

11 my work I see racism in action all the time, and Conlee's attitude showed that he was dis-

12 turbed by the sight of a young, fit, good-looking African-American driving a luxury car. He

13 didn't know anything about Clayton. He didn't know that the car was leased used. But that

14 didn't matter. To Conlee, Clayton was a black man behaving above his station, so obviously

15 he must be a drug dealer or something. Everything happened so fast, and I was so upset,

16 but I think Conlee may even have called Clayton "boy" at some point.

17

18 I remember there was some final exchange of words between Clayton and Conlee. Appar-

19 ently, when he called in Clayton's license, Conlee found out that he had stopped a state

20 trooper. I think he knew he had made a huge mistake and was going to be in hot water.

21

22 I never saw Clayton show the officers his police badge or police ID, or tell them he was

23 a state trooper until Conlee asked him. I never saw Conlee or Parsell take their guns

24 out of their holsters, but Parsell had his hand on his gun and I was afraid for Clayton's

25 safety—I think anyone would be, given the number of unarmed blacks who've been shot

26 by the police.

27

28 After we drove away, Clayton pulled over and called his supervisor. I heard Clayton say

29 that he had been pulled over because he was black—the exact conclusion I had drawn.

30 When the call ended, Clayton became very quiet, and I could tell from his facial expression

1   that he was really, really upset. I know that it's best to say nothing when Clayton gets this

2   way; he needs time alone to process his emotions. People think all state troopers are ma-

3   cho types, but Clayton is a sensitive soul. Clayton told me that he wasn't hungry and that

4   he would just drop me off at my mother's house.

5

6   I called Clayton the next day. He was very agitated. He said that the only reason we were

7   stopped was because of the color of our skin. I agreed. Over the next several weeks,

8   Clayton was irritable, moody, and avoided family time. He was less affectionate, less in-

9   timate. He complained of migraine headaches and nausea, and would sit alone in a dark

10   room. Clayton was a skinny guy to begin with; he didn't need to be losing weight from

11   not eating, but it was just falling off of him. I begged him to go see a doctor. It took a while

12   to convince him, but once Clayton started seeing Dr. Collins, he gradually began to get

13   better. Even with all that assistance, it was a full year after the incident before Clayton

14   was back to normal.

15

16   Exhibit 15 is a true and accurate copy of excerpts from my Facebook page, including the

17   post I made on August 6, YR-2, after talking to Clayton on the phone. I was furious that

18   our special day together was ruined by a terrifying and degrading instance of race dis-

19   crimination. Given our positions, both Clayton and I felt a special responsibility to take

20   action in response to such blatant racism.

I have read this deposition, and the answers are true to the best of my knowledge and belief.

/s/Shelley Elliot
Shelley Elliot
Date: December 28, YR-1

/s/Nicole Brennen
Nicole Brennen
Notary Public

DEPOSITION OF NELSON DIGBY

1   I am currently a sergeant at the Lewistown station of the Nita State Police. I am Caucasian.

2   In August of YR-2, I was the station commander at the Barrington station of the Nita State

3   Police, where Clayton Stucky was assigned as a trooper. I had been Trooper Stucky's super-

4   visor for a year and five months at that time.

5

6   I have been a law enforcement officer for twenty-four years. Before I became a supervisor,

7   I spent five years as a trooper and nine years as a corporal. In both positions, my primary

8   duties involved patrolling and enforcing traffic laws on the Nita Turnpike.

9

10   On August 5, YR-2, sometime before lunch, I received a call from Trooper Stucky. He was

11   very upset and agitated. He said he had just had been stopped by the Nita City Police and

12   the officer would not tell him why he was being stopped. I could hear a female crying in

13   the background as well as a male voice. Trooper Stucky did not ask me to talk to the police

14   officers or to intercede in the stop. I told Trooper Stucky to do whatever the officers asked

15   and to call me back when the incident was over. I told him I would report the stop to the

16   Nita City Police Chief. The phone call with Clayton lasted two or three minutes.

17

18   I called Nita City Police Chief Lieber and told him that two of his officers had stopped

19   one of my officers for a traffic violation. I stated that Trooper Stucky claimed that

20   there was no basis for the stop. I may or may not have related that Trooper Stucky was

21   African-American. I told Chief Lieber that I wasn't asking him to intervene in the inci-

22   dent, but simply was making him aware of the situation. Chief Lieber thanked me for

23   calling and said he would follow up with the officers. I never heard from Chief Lieber,

24   nor did I call him to ask about what he did after my call.

25

26   At some time within the next hour, I received a second call from Trooper Stucky. He said

27   that the officers had given him a citation claiming he had been driving fifty-five miles

28   per hour. He said that he had been driving at the speed limit. Trooper Stucky was very

1   agitated and said that the only reason the officers had stopped him because he was an

2   African-American driving a Lexus, and had used the stop as an excuse to try to search

3   his car.

4

5   Unless an officer receives a reliable description identifying that a suspect is of a certain

6   race, race should never be used as a basis for law enforcement action. The Nita State

7   Police has specific, statewide training programs to train our officers on avoiding racial

8   profiling. I am not familiar with the training programs offered by local police depart-

9   ments in the State of Nita. Nita State Police officers also will not issue speeding citations,

10 including citations for driving at an unreasonable speed under Section 3361 of the Nita

11 Motor Vehicle Code, unless the speed of the vehicle has been obtained using a calibrated

12 speed timing device. The only time the Nita State Police issue a citation for violation of

13 Section 3361 without a calibrated speed timing device is in the event of a collision. If a

14 Nita State Trooper issued a citation for violation of Section 3361 based only on a naked

15 eye observation of the speed of the vehicle on a roadway that is wet, I would tell the

16 Trooper to withdraw or discharge the citation.

17

18 Trooper Stucky never indicated that he showed the officers his badge and identification

19 to induce them to drop the charges. Had Trooper Stucky attempted to use his office to

20 obtain favorable treatment, I would have written him up for violating Nita State Police

21 regulations. Trooper Stucky never indicated to me in either phone call that he feared for

22 his safety during the stop.

23

24 If a trooper receives a traffic citation, he is required to report that citation to his supervisor.

25 If found guilty of the violation, the trooper may receive disciplinary action from the state

26 police—typically a reprimand for a first offense. Of course, punishment for subsequent

27 misconduct could be stiffer if a state police officer already has a reprimand on his record.

28

29 I observed changes in Trooper Stucky's behavior after the August traffic stop. He seemed

30 tired and became quieter and less happy. Trooper Stucky lost weight—he was skinny to

1 begin with, so the weight loss was not healthy. Trooper Stucky's reports contained more

2 errors, and his general productivity decreased markedly. A couple of other officers came

3 to me to express their concern over changes in Trooper Stucky's behavior and physical

4 condition. I became concerned enough to refer Trooper Stucky to the Nita State Police

5 Members Assistance Program, where troopers are specifically assigned to assist other

6 troopers with personal problems and perhaps to give guidance as to where to seek help.

7

8 This was not the first time I recommended the program to Trooper Stucky. In June of

9 YR-3, Trooper Stucky was very stressed in connection with a grand jury investigation

10 of allegations that he had taken personal possession of drugs seized in a traffic stop.

11 The allegations ultimately were determined to be unfounded and no adverse employ-

12 ment action was taken against Trooper Stucky, but his productivity declined during the

13 investigation, and he repeatedly called in sick. I thought the program could help Trooper

14 Stucky cope with the stress of the investigation, but do not know whether he ever sought

15 counseling through the program then or after the August YR-2 incident.

16

17 Trooper Stucky took a medical leave in March or April of YR-1. His appearance, behavior,

18 and work performance improved over the summer of YR-1. I was transferred to the Lew-

19 istown station in July of YR-1 and have not seen or spoken to Trooper Stucky since then.

I have read this deposition, and the answers are true to the best of my knowledge and belief.

/s/ *Nelson Digby*
Nelson Digby
Date: October 21, YR-1

/s/ *Thomas Place*
Thomas Place
Notary Public

DEPOSITION OF ERIC CONLEE

1 I am sixty-one years old. I have been married to my wife Sharon for thirty years. We like

2 to travel and have a large collection of birds. We have no children.

3

4 I dropped out of high school in the eleventh grade and enlisted in the United States

5 Army. I served in a field artillery battery unit in Germany. After re-enlisting, I went

6 to the military police school at Fort Gordon, Georgia, and then was selected for the

7 military police honor guard at Arlington National Cemetery. I served a tour of duty

8 in Germany as an MP. After my term of enlistment ended, I received an honorary dis-

9 charge. I briefly worked as a prison guard at the Nita County prison, and then became

10 a police officer for Nita Township for twenty-seven years. For the first half of my career

11 I did everything—criminal work and motor vehicle work. As time went on, I preferred

12 working the motor vehicle laws and was promoted to corporal, after which I pretty

13 much ran the traffic program. There was no field training program, so I went to the

14 chief of police and asked him if I could develop a training program. He allowed me to

15 go ahead and I put together the training program on motor vehicle enforcement that

16 the township still uses.

17

18 I joined the Nita City Police Department in October of YR-6, after retiring with a full

19 pension from the Nita Township Police Department. I did so both because I missed po-

20 lice work, and also because I lost a great deal of money in a failed real estate deal that

21 was secured by my pension from Nita Township, so I needed to keep working to make

22 ends meet.

23

24 When I was in junior high and high school, I played on the football, baseball, and basket-

25 ball teams, all of which included African-Americans. When I was fourteen, my first girl-

26 friend was African-American. She later died in a car crash. All through my Army career,

27 I had friends and supervisors who were African-American. When I was in Germany, my

28 first two sergeants were African-Americans. I also played pick-up basketball in Nita for

1   many years, and often would go to play in areas where I was the only Caucasian player.

2   I also serve as an umpire at amateur fast and slow pitch leagues, and am often teamed

3   up with umpires who are African-American.

4

5   My understanding is that you should never base any traffic stop on someone's race or

6   ethnic group. Absolutely never. First of all, it's not right. It's not the way I was brought up.

7   You know, I'm an American—that's the way I believe someone should act. Although I have

8   never received any formal training on racial profiling, I certainly knew what I could and

9   couldn't do, and I know in my heart what I would and wouldn't do. When I was hired by

10 the Nita City Police, I received a manual. Section 2 of the manual includes a Code of Ethics

11 that reads:

12

13   In order for the office to be successful in meeting its responsibilities, it is vitally

14   important to first obtain the respect and confidence of people. Such desirable

15   attitudes can be cultivated only by the efforts of each individual officer through

16   his or her daily contact with the public. The principles set forth in this code of

17   conduct are predicated upon the pronouncements found in the law and enforce-

18   ment code of ethics and police officer's oath of office.

19

20 Section 2.01 of the manual constitutes the code of ethics and states, "above all else I shall

21 respect the constitutional rights of all men and women to liberty, equality, and justice."

22 Section 2.02 of the manual is the oath of office, which states, "I will support, obey, and

23 defend the Constitution of the United States and the State of Nita." The manual does not

24 specifically refer to the issue of racial profiling or the use of race or ethnicity as a basis for

25 law enforcement action.

26

27 When I was hired, Chief Lieber met with me and told me that he expected me to treat

28 everybody equally and to be fair and do the best job that I possibly can. Chief Lieber has

29 very high standards. The manual and Chief Lieber's instructions were basically the same

30 instructions I had received when I was in service with Nita Township.

1   My primary duties with Nita City were courtroom security and transporting prisoners.

2   I did both short-range transports, from the Nita County prison to the Nita County Court-

3   house, as well as long-range transports taking prisoners to state correctional institutions

4   throughout the state. During the long-range transports, I often would pay for snacks for

5   the prisoners out of my own pocket. Many of the prisoners were African-American or

6   Hispanic.

7

8   I missed the excitement of on-the-road policing and believed that Chief Lieber was not

9   taking full advantage of my skills and experience. Because I had twenty-five years' ex-

10   perience in traffic enforcement, I approached Chief Lieber and offered to train Nita City

11   Police officers on issuing citations for violation of the Motor Vehicle Code. I created a

12   one-week training program and wrote a manual to be distributed to officers undergoing

13   the training. Exhibit 16 is a true and correct copy of that manual.

14

15   The first day of training is in the classroom, and the remaining four training days are

16   spent out on the road. The training manual does not include any specific reference to

17   racial profiling nor avoiding the use of race or ethnicity as a basis for a traffic stop, but

18   does include the verbatim text of the code of ethics that appears in the general office

19   manual. During the classroom training, I discuss the requirements of the code of ethics

20   and the requirement of probable cause to make a traffic stop. My training manual and

21   training program do not include instruction on using traffic stops to develop probable

22   cause that the driver may be engaged in activity that violates the criminal code. The goal

23   is to train officers to write a basic traffic citation and teach them enough of the Motor

24   Vehicle Code to do the job properly; experience will expand that basic knowledge as they

25   go along.

26

27   The five-day traffic training program for Nita City officers that began on August 4, YR-2

28   was the ninth or tenth that I've taught. The first day was spent entirely in the classroom.

29   On August 5, I was on the road in the late morning training Officer Parsell. I had never

30   worked directly with Parsell before. He was assigned to the Protection from Abuse Unit.

1   We left the station around 11:45 for on-the-road training. Parsell and I were driving a

2   marked police car and both of us were in uniform. Anyone driving on the roadway could

3   clearly see that we were police officers.

4

5   I turned right onto Market Street from South Pine, driving in the left, eastbound travel

6   lane. The speed limit there is twenty-five miles per hour. It was raining fairly hard. We

7   pulled up to the red light at the corner of East Market and Broad Street. I may have

8   noticed the Lexus out of the corner of my eye, but did not turn to see the driver and

9   certainly did not know the race of the persons in the car.

10

11   After the light turned green, I proceeded forward on Market Street. I was traveling

12   about twenty-five miles per hour. I could see—in my right, side-view mirror or rear

13   view mirror—the Lexus approaching our car in the right lane. It was moving at a high

14   rate of speed—I estimate at about fifty or fifty-five miles per hour. The Lexus passed

15   our police car on the right. As it passed, I instantaneously determined that the car was

16   traveling well in excess of the posted speed limit. While the objective on this day was

17   not to train Officer Parsell in estimating speed, either with his naked eye or with a

18   speed timing device, I could not ignore Mr. Stucky's unlawful driving. I told Officer Par-

19   sell, "He looks like he's going at least fifty miles per hour. That is a good example of

20   driving at an unsafe speed." Parsell agreed. I sped up, pulled into the right lane behind

21   the Lexus, and activated the overhead lights. Mr. Stucky initially moved his car to the

22   left lane, but when I pulled my car behind him again, he immediately pulled over to the

23   left parking lane of the road.

24

25   In order to have probable cause to stop Mr. Stucky for speeding in violation of Sec-

26   tion 3362 of the Motor Vehicle Code, we would have had to determine his speed by using

27   a calibrated electronic speed device or by tracking his speed for 3/10 of a mile using a

28   calibrated speedometer on the car. Because I was not training Officer Parsell on the use of

29   radar on August 5, YR-2, we did not have the radar gun in the patrol car. We did not track

30   Stucky's speed for 3/10 of a mile before activating the overhead lights on the police car

1   because I was not citing him for speeding, but rather for violating Section 3361, driving at

2   an unreasonable speed under the conditions.

3

4   This was the first citation for violation of Section 3361 I issued since joining the Nita

5   City Police Department. I am only on the road issuing citations when I am training new

6   officers. My review of the police records indicates I have issued around 100 traffic ci-

7   tations since joining the Nita City Police—eight of which were to African-Americans.

8   I have not issued a citation for violation of 3361 while on the road training officers

9   since I stopped Mr. Stucky. A review of all citations issued by the Nita City Police from

10 YR-6 to YR-2 indicates that citations for violation of 3361 were only issued twice,

11 other than the stop of Mr. Stucky.

12

13 The two variables that gave rise to the stop were the weather conditions and the speed

14 at which Mr. Stucky was driving his car. I determined with my naked eye that Stucky was

15 driving around fifty to fifty-five miles per hour. At the time of the stop, I had been a police

16 officer for thirty-one years. I have been doing this for so long that I am not like your nor-

17 mal police officer; I just compute things a lot quicker. I never took a course that specifically

18 trained me to estimate speed without use of a scientific device. I did, however, take cours-

19 es in which we used electronic devices such as VASCAR to determine speed. You can't just

20 time every car on the road when you're sitting on the highway; these devices require you

21 to make a judgment that a car is speeding as it approaches a reference point so that you

22 activate the device. I also am certified to use a device called Accutrack, which is kind of an

23 advanced stopwatch that also requires that you get an idea of how fast a vehicle is going as

24 it approaches a reference point. I have never been accepted by a court as an expert witness

25 to testify as to the speed of a car when I was not also using a device that measures speed.

26

27 As the narrative portion of the citation indicates, the conditions that made the speed un-

28 reasonable were the rain and a wet roadway. When we left the station at 11:45, it was

29 raining hard enough that we ran to the vehicle. We did not bring or retrieve our rain gear

30 from our lockers. I did not feel that it was going to rain all day. The rain started to taper

1   when we stopped Mr. Stucky. I did not need to return to the station to change my uniform

2   following issuance of the citation to Mr. Stucky.

3

4   Officer Parsell used the radio and called the stop in to the radio controller at headquar-

5   ters. I approached the driver's side window of the Lexus and, after he left the patrol car,

6   told Officer Parsell to assume the proper guarding position at the rear passenger side

7   of the car. I saw Mr. Stucky in the driver's seat and a woman in the front passenger seat.

8   I did not observe that the driver of the Lexus was African-American until I walked up

9   to the driver's side window after making the stop. The training manual I prepared does

10   instruct the officer "from the moment you decide to stop a vehicle, it is very important

11   that you closely observe any movements or actions by the occupants of the vehicles you

12   are stopping." Observing these movements is important because it might alert you to the

13   possibility of an attack or that the occupants are trying to conceal evidence.

14

15   I asked for his license and registration and then told Mr. Stucky that he had been driving at

16   an unreasonable speed for the conditions, fifty or fifty-five miles an hour when the road-

17   ways are wet. Mr. Stucky denied that he was driving that fast, but did not tell me how fast

18   he was going. He reached over and picked up a cell phone. I said, "Sir, would you please put

19   down the cell phone and give me your driver's license and registration." He totally ignored

20   me. Stucky looked straight ahead and dialed a number on the cell phone. I knew the call

21   was answered because Mr. Stucky was talking and listening, clearly in a conversation with

22   someone. I could not really hear what he was saying. Again I asked him to put the cell phone

23   down and give me his license and registration, and again he ignored me. I must have asked

24   him for his license and registration, and to put down the cell phone, five to seven times;

25   each time he totally ignored me until he laid the cell phone down on the seat. I always ad-

26   dressed Stucky as "sir," and my tone of voice was normal. I was never yelling and never loud.

27

28   At that point, I grew suspicious that Mr. Stucky was carrying drugs in his car. While

29   I was not training Officer Parsell on drug detection, from my almost thirty years of law

30   enforcement experience I know that one always must be alert to objective signs that

1   a person stopped for a motor vehicle violation is involved in a more serious offense.

2   I made several drug arrests arising out of traffic stops when I worked at Nita Township.

3   While it did not occur to me at the time, making a drug bust could have encouraged Chief

4   Lieber to put me back on the street. At my request, Mr. Stucky showed me the contents

5   of a camera bag and backpack in the back seat of the car. However, Stucky's demeanor

6   suddenly changed when I asked for permission to look in the trunk. He refused to open

7   the trunk and then quickly retrieved his registration from the glove box and handed me

8   the registration and his license. The woman in the passenger seat did not say a word and

9   barely looked at me. At no point was she ever crying.

10

11   At some point, Officer Parsell came up to the driver's side of the car. I told Officer Parsell

12   to stay with Stucky's car and returned to the police car with Mr. Stucky's license and regis-

13   tration. I believed Stucky had drugs in the trunk of his car due to his hostile demeanor, his

14   type of clothing, and the sudden withdrawal of consent to search once I asked to search

15   the trunk, so I intended to ask the dispatcher to send out an officer with the drug dog to

16   sniff the exterior of the car. Before I could radio that request, I received a call from dis-

17   patch indicating that Chief Lieber wanted to see us about our stop of a state trooper. That

18   was the first indication I had that Stucky might be a police officer. I told the dispatcher

19   that we would report back to the station once we were done. I did not request a drug

20   dog—just wrote up the citation.

21

22   When I walked back to the car, I asked Stucky whether he would sign to acknowledge the

23   citation, and he said, "No way." The motorist is not under any legal obligation to sign the

24   citation. Stucky then said, "I know the drill. Don't you extend the privilege to a brother," or

25   something like that. I said, "Are you a police officer?" He answered yes. I then said some-

26   thing to the effect that, "If you are a police officer, you're the first person in that profession

27   that's ever been disrespectful to me in this manner."

28

29   I have pulled over many police officers in my career. Many of these officers were persons

30   of color. Most officers will show me a badge or an ID. Our own department policy and

1   our policy manual prohibit us from showing our badge if we are stopped for a traffic

2   violation. The Nita State Police have the same policy. I can't say that it is proper, but most

3   professions take care of each other. There is a brotherhood among police as well. If I find

4   out I have stopped a police officer, I let them go without issuing a citation. But I cited

5   Mr. Stucky because of the way he treated me, his conduct, everything; it just appalled me.

6   If Mr. Stucky had just shown me his badge when I came up to the car window, I would not

7   have issued him a citation. I wish he had just shown me his badge right off the bat; we

8   would not be here today.

9

10 After issuing the citation to Stucky, Officer Parsell and I immediately returned to the sta-

11 tion to see Chief Lieber. While I never even thought about Stucky's race in connection with

12 the stop, I was aware that I would be fired if Chief Lieber concluded I had stopped Stucky

13 based on his race. However, I thought the reason Chief Lieber wanted to see us was so that

14 he could report Stucky's inexcusable conduct to the state police. Chief Lieber asked what

15 exactly had occurred. Both Officer Parsell and I told Chief Lieber what had happened

16 during the stop. No one said anything about Stucky's race during the meeting with Chief

17 Lieber. Chief Lieber said that he has never interfered with another officer's citation, so he

18 left the decision up to me whether to withdraw or to continue to prosecute the citation.

19 I indicated that I did not want to withdraw the citation because of Mr. Stucky's abusive

20 behavior during the stop.

21

22 In my twenty-seven years with Nita Township, I never received any complaints of a racial

23 nature. I did receive periodic written performance evaluations when I worked for Nita

24 Township. We are ranked by our captain in various categories. The levels of ranking for

25 each category are "outstanding," when the officer always displays the characteristic, "good,"

26 when the officer displays the characteristic more than average, and "average," where the

27 officer usually displays the characteristic. One of the categories on which we were ranked

28 was whether the officer conducts himself with "lack of prejudice." In the sixteen years

29 in which I was evaluated for the category of lack of prejudice, I never received a ranking

30

1   of "outstanding," but I received a ranking of "good" four times and received a ranking of

2   "average" twelve times. Exhibit 17 is true and accurate copies of my written performance

3   evaluations from Nita Township for the category "lack of prejudice."

4

5   Since I have been working at the Nita City Police Department, I have never had a com-

6   plaint that I have treated someone wrongly based on their race or ethnicity, other than

7   the claim made by Mr. Stucky.

8

9   In August of YR-3, Chief Lieber had disciplined me for an incident arising out of my trans-

10 port of four inmates from the prison to the courthouse. The four prisoners were locked

11 in a van that I was driving. When I arrived at the courthouse, I was supposed to go to the

12 cell block and log the prisoners in on an intake sheet, and a deputy sheriff would come

13 out and take the prisoners from the van. I walked into the cell block and immediately

14 turned in my paperwork. I was in a hurry, so while I assumed that the deputy sheriffs

15 were going to take the prisoners out, I did not stay there and be sure they did so as is re-

16 quired. Instead, I went about my other duties at the courthouse, and later found out that

17 the inmates remained locked in my van for a couple of hours until another deputy heard

18 someone screaming from inside the van. Two of the inmates were African-American, and

19 the other two were Hispanic. I felt really bad, because I knew that it was warm and they

20 were in the van, and I thank God that nobody in there got sick or any other harm came

21 to them. It was kind of devastating to me because nothing like that had ever happened

22 to me ever before, and it really, really shook me and like I said, it was all my fault. Chief

23 Lieber suspended me for six days without pay for the incident, which was one level of

24 discipline shy of being fired. Chief Lieber told me that I would be fired if I had one more

25 flagrant violation.

26

27 Two months later, in October of YR-3, I was suspended for two days. I was working in

28 the courthouse, and I came down into the area where we would process newly convicted

29 inmates to be taken to the county prison. I searched a Hispanic individual named Luis

30

1   Alcevedo. I took off his jewelry, belt, and wallet, did an inventory of the objects, and put

2   them in an envelope on which I signed my name. When we get to the prison, they check

3   the inventory against the contents of the envelope. We had a memo that said you were

4   supposed to staple the envelope. Due to an oversight on my part, I did not staple the en-

5   velope. I put Alcevedo in the transport van and put the envelope on the front seat. When

6   we arrived at the Nita County prison, the envelope at some point must have been turned

7   upside down, and all the weight from the belt and everything went to the bottom, which

8   caused the sides to balloon out, and somehow the watch slipped out of the envelope and

9   onto the pavement. I did not realize that had happened. I took Alcevedo and what I be-

10   lieved to be all his personal property to the Nita County prison and turned the envelope in

11   to the people inside the prison. Instead of waiting for Alcevedo's property to be logged in

12   and inventoried, I went to lunch. When I came back, they brought it to my attention that a

13   watch was missing. I went back out to where I had parked the van in the parking lot to see

14   if I could find the watch. I saw the watch lying in a garbage can—apparently it had been

15   run over and for all practical purposes was destroyed. Supposedly, the watch was worth

16    $1,000. Chief Lieber was not on duty when the report of the incident occurred, and I was

17   suspended by my immediate supervisor, Assistant Chief Levenger. I do not know whether

18   Assistant Chief Levenger ever made Chief Lieber aware of the suspension.

19

20   Both Officer Parsell and I testified about the circumstances of the stop at the trial on

21   Mr. Stucky's traffic citation before the municipal judge. The judge ruled that we had not

22   proved beyond a reasonable doubt that Mr. Stucky was guilty of violating Section 3361.

23   I was shocked by the decision. While the judge stated that she was appalled by Stucky's

24   suggestion of racial profiling, I suspect she figured that with all the controversies raging

25   across the country, it was not in her interest to inflame the situation and make a martyr

26   of Stucky by finding Stucky guilty.

I have read this deposition, and the answers are true to the best of my knowledge and belief.

/s/Eric Conlee
Eric Conlee
Date: August 13, YR-1

/s/Camille Marion
Camille Marion
Notary Public

Deposition of Lance Parsell

1   I am twenty-seven years old and live at 238 Devonshire Road, Nita. I am married and have

2   a three-year-old child. I went to high school at the Christian School of Nita, and received

3   my associate's degree in Criminal Justice at Nita Area Community College. I then worked

4   for Sears for a couple of years as a manager, and I have been employed by the Nita City

5   Police Department since March of YR-2.

6

7   When I was hired at the Nita City Police Department, I received a manual containing a

8   code of ethics and oath of office. Both the code of ethics and the oath require that officers

9   treat all individuals fairly, equally, and impartially. There is no specific reference to racial

10 profiling or the use of race as a basis for law enforcement action in the manual. When

11 I was hired, Chief Lieber called me into his office and told me he expected that I would

12 always treat members of the public fairly and with respect.

13

14 My first few months of work involved courtroom security, transporting prisoners, and

15 working in the pistol permit office. I then did a stint in the Protection From Abuse unit,

16 serving protection orders.

17

18 Sometime in the second week of July YR-2, Sergeant Gable assigned me to attend traffic

19 enforcement training. Officer Conlee gave me a traffic manual to read and study before

20 our on-the-road training. I read the manual in its entirety. There is no specific reference

21 to racial profiling or the use of race as a basis for a traffic stop in the manual. The manual

22 did not include any information on expanding the traffic stop into a criminal investigation

23 beyond the requirement that during the stop, we must report the driver's license, license

24 number, and registration to the station.

25

26 On Monday, July 25, YR-2, I attended a class with six other new officers taught by Officer

27 Conlee in which he went over the manual with us. I had not met or worked with Officer

28 Conlee before the traffic training.

1   On Tuesday, August 5, YR-2, I was being trained on making traffic stops with Officer

2   Conlee. The purpose of the training was to practice writing citations and to learn the

3   fundamentals of the Motor Vehicle Code.

4

5   We left the police station at about 11:45 to begin the on-the-road training. We were

6   using a marked Crown Victoria police car, with the emblem of the department on the

7   side and a standard light bar on top. The Nita City Police Department does not equip its

8   cars with cameras to record interactions with citizens. Both Officer Conlee and I were

9   in full police uniform. I was in the passenger seat of the patrol car, and Officer Conlee

10   was driving.

11

12   I first noticed Mr. Stucky's car, a late model Lexus, sitting in the travel lane to the right of

13   us at the stop light at the 400 block of East Market Street where it intersects with Broad

14   Street. I did notice that he was African-American and that the woman in the passenger

15   seat also was a person of color. The driver did not turn to look at our car, which I found to

16   be very unusual and even suspicious, as if he were trying to avoid eye contact.

17

18   The speed limit on East Market Street at that point is twenty-five miles per hour. When

19   the traffic light turned green, we proceeded down East Market Street driving at the

20   twenty-five miles per hour speed limit. Within less than a block, Mr. Stucky's Lexus

21   roared past us in the right lane. Officer Conlee stated, "He looks like he is going fifty or

22   fifty-five miles an hour." While I have not taken any courses in estimating speed with

23   the naked eye and had not looked at the speedometer of our patrol car, Officer Conlee's

24   estimate seemed accurate to me, and I concurred with that. Officer Conlee then stated,

25   "This is a good example of a safe speed violation, we are going to ticket that vehicle."

26   Officer Conlee immediately flipped on the overhead lights, and pulled Stucky's car over.

27   Mr. Stucky did not try to get away, and pulled over to the left side of the road once Offi-

28   cer Conlee activated the overhead lights. I have no idea why Mr. Stucky would drive fifty

29   miles per hour in a twenty-five mile per hour zone past a marked police car—maybe he

30   was trying to impress the girl in the passenger seat.

1   We stopped Mr. Stucky at around 11:50 a.m. because we had probable cause that he had

2   violated Section 3361 of the Nita Motor Vehicle Code, which prohibits driving at an un-

3   reasonable speed under the conditions. I radioed county control to give them the location

4   of our stop and the license plate of the vehicle. Officer Conlee walked up to the driver's

5   side window, and I assumed the proper guarding position at the right rear of the vehicle.

6

7   I observed Officer Conlee and Mr. Stucky talking, but could not hear the conversation

8   because of the passing traffic on the road. I did not hear any shouting. I never heard the

9   passenger in the car crying. I was surprised that Mr. Stucky did not immediately hand

10 over his license and registration, and even more surprised when I saw him pick up his cell

11 phone and appear to be talking to someone.

12

13 While I did not hear what Mr. Stucky was saying, it was obvious from where I was standing

14 that he considered the circumstances of the stop to be inappropriate. I noticed that Officer

15 Conlee had a frustrated look on his face, so I walked over to stand next to Officer Conlee at

16 the driver's side window. I did not notice any evidence that the passenger was upset. She

17 seemed fine. Officer Conlee repeatedly asked Mr. Stucky for his license and registration.

18 At some point I saw Mr. Stucky reach into the glove compartment of his car and retrieve

19 some paperwork and hand it to Officer Conlee. I never heard Mr. Stucky identify himself as

20 a police officer or display his state police badge or identification. I never heard Mr. Stucky

21 speaking other than in a normal tone, use profanity, or make any derogatory comments.

22

23 Because Mr. Stucky's refusal to cooperate and making the phone call aroused our suspi-

24 cion, Officer Conlee asked Mr. Stucky for permission to look in two bags that were in the

25 rear seat of the car. Probably because he knew there was nothing illegal in those bags,

26 Mr. Stucky consented to those searches. But as soon as Conlee asked him to pop the

27 trunk, Mr. Stucky became nervous and flustered, as if he had something to hide. I believe

28 Mr. Stucky's conduct gave us reasonable suspicion that he was concealing contraband in

29 the trunk, but Officer Conlee did not pursue the search any further. I think he had a sixth

30 sense that Mr. Stucky was trying to bait him into escalating the situation.

1   I remained at the driver's side window when Officer Conlee walked back to the patrol

2   car to call in the driver's license and write up the citations. When Officer Conlee walked

3   back to Mr. Stucky's car and handed him the citations, Mr. Stucky said, "I know the drill.

4   Don't you extend any courtesy to a brother?" Officer Conlee asked if Mr. Stucky was

5   a police officer, and Mr. Stucky indicated that he did work for the state police. Officer

6   Conlee said something about how Mr. Stucky's actions were beneath the dignity of a

7   police officer.

8

9   When I returned to the police car, Officer Conlee told me that while he was in the car

10 writing the citation, he received a dispatch indicating that Chief Lieber wanted us to re-

11 turn to the station to discuss our stopping a state police officer. We chatted about the

12 circumstances of the stop, agreed that we did not do anything wrong, and then began our

13 return to the station. Officer Conlee did not mention anything about having previously

14 been disciplined by Chief Lieber, but I did notice concern on his face as we drove back to

15 the station.

16

17 While we were en route, I texted my fellow officer, Bethany Paget, who was at the police

18 station, to see if she had heard any reason why Chief Lieber had called us back to the

19 station. Exhibit 18 is a true and accurate copy of my text message. Bethany texted back

20 immediately, indicating she had no information about why Chief Lieber had called us in.

21 Exhibit 19 is a true and accurate copy of her reply. "NFI" stands for "no fucking idea."

22 I apologize for the inappropriate language we both used in our messages. We have a

23 tendency to use "locker room talk" that we would never use outside the station.

24

25 Officer Conlee and I went together to Chief Lieber's office. Chief Lieber asked us what

26 happened out on the road. Chief Lieber did not seem mad, just curious. I listened

27 to Officer Conlee describe the circumstances of the stop. I heard Officer Conlee say,

28 "I didn't even know the driver was black until we approached the car." While I had

29 seen the race of the driver when we were stopped at the light, I did not know what

30 Officer Conlee did or did not see, so I did not tell Chief Lieber that I knew before the stop

1   that the driver was black. But I certainly did not tell Chief Lieber that I was unaware

2   that the driver was black. Mr. Stucky's race had nothing to do with this traffic stop.

3

4   There is a separate offense under the Motor Vehicle Code for driving in excess of the

5   speed limit, Section 3362. In order to cite someone for speeding under Section 3362, we

6   would need to use either a mechanical speed device, such as radar, or a speedometer in

7   the patrol car that has been tested and calibrated as accurate within a certain time period

8   before the stop. In addition, to use the speedometer as a basis for determining the speed,

9   the Motor Vehicle Code requires that we track the speed of the vehicle for three-tenths of

10   a mile. The requirement to track the speed for three-tenths of a mile ensures that some-

11   one has not just had a momentary lapse and just happened to go over the speed limit then

12   resumed a legal speed.

13

14   The patrol car we were driving had a calibrated speedometer, but we did not have radar

15   with us that day, as we were training on making traffic stops while on moving patrol as

16   opposed to sitting on the side of the road measuring speed with a radar gun. We did not

17   track the speed of the car for three-tenths of a mile before activating the overhead lights.

18   Because we did not track his speed for three-tenths of a mile with our speedometer, nor

19   used a radar gun, we did not have cause to stop Stucky for violating Section 3362, though

20   I personally think he was driving twenty-five to thirty miles per hour over the speed limit.

21

22   We did not observe Stucky swerving toward any parked cars to his right or swerving out

23   of his lane. While he was speeding, Stucky never lost control of his car. We did not issue

24   Stucky a citation for reckless driving or for following too close to another vehicle.

25

26   In order to stop a motorist for violating Section 3361, there must be some condition that

27   makes the speed unsafe. The narrative portion of the citation we issued indicates the

28   conditions that made the speed unsafe—rain and a wet roadway. At the time of the stop,

29   there was a light rain falling. As part of our standard uniform, we are issued rain gear

30   to wear over our uniform to repel the rain. We did not bring our rain gear to the patrol

1 car when we left the police station. Even though I was out of the patrol car for around

2 thirty minutes during the stop, I did not need to change into a new uniform after the

3 stop because it had stopped raining during the stop.

4

5 I had never stopped a driver for violating Section 3361 before this stop. I have not

6 stopped someone for violating Section 3361 since the stop of Mr. Stucky. Mr. Stucky was

7 the only African-American to whom we issued a traffic citation during the three days

8 I was involved in on-the-road training with Officer Conlee.

9

10 Both Officer Conlee and I testified at the hearing on the traffic citation before the mu-

11 nicipal judge. Following the hearing, the judge found Mr. Stucky not guilty of violating

12 Section 3361. I remain assigned to the Protection from Abuse unit. While I successfully

13 completed the traffic enforcement training, Chief Lieber has not assigned me to police the

14 roadways. I suspect that he does not want to do anything that would unfairly prejudice

15 his defense in this lawsuit.

I have read this deposition, and the answers are true to the best of my knowledge and belief.

/s/Lance Parsell
Lance Parsell
Date: August 13, YR-1

/s/Camille Marion
Camille Marion
Notary Public

DEPOSITION OF KURT LIEBER

1   I am happily married and have three children. I have an associate's degree in police

2   science and administration from Nita Community College. I have been the Chief of

3   Police of the Nita City Police Department since YR-18. Before becoming chief, I was

4   an officer with the Department for eighteen years. I am affiliated with the National

5   Association of Police Chiefs and the Nita Chief of Police Association. I have served and

6   continue to serve on the advisory board of the Nita City Human Relations Commission.

7

8   I belong to several personal organizations as well: the VFW, the American Legion, the

9   Rooster Social Club, the Vigilant Club, the Prince Athletic Association, and the 13th Ward

10   Political Club. The Rooster Social Club is a club where guys get together, a stag club. No

11   African-Americans are members of the club. There is at least one Latino member. The 13th

12   Ward Political Club and the Prince Athletic Association also are social clubs whose mem-

13   bership is limited to males. The only event I ever attended at the Prince Athletic Association

14   was their golf outing—I do not recall seeing any African-Americans at these outings.

15

16   I have ultimate hiring and firing authority for the Police Department. No one within

17   the Department or the City reviews my decisions to hire and fire. There are about

18   seventy-seven officers in the Nita City Police Department. Six of the officers are not

19   Caucasian—five African-Americans and one Latino. I just lost a Latino officer to an-

20   other department and a black officer just retired. There also is an officer, Alfie Chini,

21   who might be part Asian, but I do not ask those things. None of the African-American

22   officers have supervisory duties—all are line officers. There is no written policy in

23   the Nita City Police Department encouraging diversity or affirmative action hiring.

24   However, I personally try to encourage minorities to apply for positions with the Po-

25   lice Department. We had an opening one time in our drug division for an investigator.

26   My drug guys came in and they named three guys they would like to have, all of them

27   were white. And I said, "Did you ever think about Mike Hill," who is African-American.

28   "He is a great police officer." They said, "He never asked." I said, "Different folks ask in

1   different ways. Why don't we ask him?" I called Mike up in my office and asked him if

2   he would be interested. He got a grin from ear to ear. Subsequently, I promoted him

3   to sergeant. There are other persons of color that I promoted as well. I also started a

4   program at the inner city public schools and at the Crispus Attucks Community Center,

5   where our officers work with underprivileged kids, many of whom are minorities.

6

7   All Nita City Police Officers are required to undergo basic training from the State of Nita.

8   While the curriculum in that training does not include specific instruction on avoiding

9   racial profiling, there is a session on cultural diversity.

10

11   I set the policies regarding training and instruction for the Nita City Police Department.

12   While I may seek input from others, I do not need to seek approval from anyone else in

13   the City before instituting a policy. As Chief of Police, I implemented the current depart-

14   mental policies. My first year as chief, I developed a Nita City Police Department Policy

15   Manual, which is the primary document setting forth the policies of the Department. As

16   a condition of his or her employment, every police officer must agree to adhere to all

17   policies in the manual. Exhibit 20 is a true and accurate copy of the manual.

18

19   The Policy Manual includes a Code of Ethics. The Code of Ethics requires that every

20   one of our officers treat all people impartially, fairly, and equally. I included this Code

21   because that's the way I was brought up, plus the Constitution requires it. There is no

22   question in my mind that stopping a motorist solely because of his race would violate

23   the United States Constitution. Even if it were not in the Constitution, my personal be-

24   lief is that you treat everyone the same as you. One of my edicts in the speech I make

25   to each of my officers when they are hired is, you treat everyone the way you would

26   want yourself or a member of your family to be treated. You need to treat people with

27   dignity and respect—all people. I hired Eric Conlee and Lance Parsell to work in the

28   Nita Police Department and had the same conversation with both of them about how to

29   treat people. I have never heard any derogatory statements by my police officers about

30   anybody of any ethnicity.

1 There is no specific ban on racial profiling, bias-based policing, or singling out a person

2 based on his or her ethnicity in the Policy Manual. There is no provision of the Policy

3 Manual exclusively instructing officers not to engage in racial profiling or bias-based

4 policing. On occasion, I issue departmental directives—memos instructing officers what

5 actions to take or not to take under certain circumstances. I have never issued a directive

6 addressing a policy against bias-based policing. I think the best way to make sure your

7 officers are behaving is not to issue a bunch of policies but to get to know the officers on

8 the force and be sure they know what you expect of them.

9

10 The Policy Manual does not address enforcement of the Motor Vehicle Code. We have a

11 different manual for traffic enforcement, which was created in YR-16. The manual sets

12 forth guidelines on vehicle stops and enforcement of the Nita Vehicle Code. There is no

13 place in the document that sets forth a specific written prohibition on bias-based policing

14 or racial profiling. However Part II(A) of the traffic manual says "members of the Nita City

15 Police Department, when enforcing the Vehicle Code, shall take appropriate enforcement

16 action for violations witnessed by them, and such enforcement actions shall be accom-

17 plished in a fair, impartial, and courteous manner."

18

19 The police department does some in-house training. No field training officer is assigned to

20 train our deputies on the subject of biased-based policing. We have never conducted train-

21 ing or instruction inside the Nita City Police Department on the subject of biased-based

22 policing. None of our trainers are African-American.

23

24 The standard State of Nita motor vehicle citation form does not have a block in which the

25 officer records the race or ethnicity of the person cited. The Nita City Police Department

26 does not have a separate form on which officers record the race or ethnicity of person

27 cited for a traffic offense. Similarly, the Department does not have a form the officer must

28 fill out indicating the race or ethnicity of the person stopped where no citation is issued

29 or no arrest is made. Because our operation is not as big as the Nita State Police or the

30 Nita Township Police, we have a pretty good handle on who is doing what and how their

1   job performance is going. And if things aren't going well, we call them in and take the

2   appropriate action. We do not have any formal periodic review of police officers. The

3   Department does not have a standard review process to determine whether officers are

4   enforcing motor vehicle code violations free from bias.

5

6   After this lawsuit was filed, I asked Sergeant Lewin to go back through all the citations

7   and written warnings that Nita City Police officers issued in the past five years to deter-

8   mine the race or ethnicity of the persons who were stopped. I asked Sergeant Lewin to

9   determine race by visually looking at the driver's license photo in the State of Nita De-

10   partment of Motor Vehicles database. We can access the photos on the computer. Some

11   of the drivers were out of state, and for some you could not clearly determine race from

12   the photo or surname, which is why the race in some stops is classified as unknown.

13   Lewin compared his findings to census data on the percentages of various members

14   of ethnicity and race in the overall population in Nita County and Nita City. I do not be-

15   lieve Sergeant Lewin made any attempt to determine racial composition of the driving

16   population, as opposed to the overall population, in the City or County. Nor would Ser-

17   geant Lewin have any ability to determine from our records the race of a person stopped

18   where the officer gave only a verbal warning. Sergeant Lewin also would not be able to

19   determine from the records how many times the officer asked the motorist for consent

20   to search or conducted a search. Exhibit 21 is a true and accurate copy of the traffic study

21   Sergeant Lewin prepared.

22

23   Officer Conlee's normal assigned duties with the Nita City Police Department were

24   prison transport and courtroom security. At some point, Conlee wrote me a memo

25   requesting that I assign him to be in charge of traffic enforcement training. I had per-

26   sonally known Officer Conlee when he was a Nita Township police officer and was fa-

27   miliar with his background and years of experience in traffic enforcement. I had heard

28   that the manual he developed with Nita Township was a very good manual. I called

29   Chief Ellis at Nita Township, who was the chief when Officer Conlee was an officer, to

30   get his thoughts on putting Officer Conlee in charge of training. Chief Ellis said that

1   Officer Conlee would do a good job for us, just don't make him a supervisor. Based on

2   the manual and Chief Ellis's recommendation, I named Officer Conlee the field train-

3   ing officer for traffic enforcement for the Department. I never requested or read any

4   of Officer Conlee's written Performance Evaluation Ratings from the Nita Township

5   Police Department.

6

7   Officer Conlee prepared a traffic enforcement training manual as well as a five-day train-

8   ing program. I reviewed and approved both the manual and the training program. Neither

9   the manual nor the training program specifically addresses racial profiling or biased-

10 based policing. I never told Officer Conlee to include a reminder in the manual that our

11 Department does not engage in biased-based policing. However, the first page of Officer

12 Conlee's traffic manual is the Code of Ethics from the Policy Manual. I never told Officer

13 Conlee to include training on avoiding racial profiling in traffic stops.

14

15 Other than the claim raised in this suit by Mr. Stucky, I have never received any com-

16 plaints from any minority, including African-Americans, that Officer Parsell or Officer

17 Conlee had mistreated them because of their race or ethnicity. About one year before

18 the stop of Mr. Stucky, I did discipline Officer Conlee for leaving four inmates locked in

19 his transport van. Two of the inmates were Hispanic and two were African-American.

20 However, there was never any indication that the inmates were left in the van because

21 of their race or ethnicity. There was an investigation of the incident, which included in-

22 terviewing the four prisoners, none of whom complained that Officer Conlee had acted

23 based on their race or ethnicity. However, this was a very serious problem. I suspended

24 Officer Conlee for six days without pay, a level four punishment, which was one level of

25 punishment shy of termination. I am ultimately responsible for supervision, monitoring,

26 and review of police officers in the Department. No one in the Department or the City

27 has the power to review my disciplinary decisions. I told Officer Conlee that I cannot put

28 up with this kind of stuff and that the next time any flagrant incident happened he was

29 no longer going to be with the Police Department. Officer Conlee understood that he was

30 one major incident away from being fired.

1   I subsequently learned that, two months later, Officer Conlee received two more one-day

2   suspensions without pay after he lost the property of an inmate, Juan Alcevedo. This was

3   a level three punishment. I was away at a conference outside the office when this incident

4   happened, and the punishment was issued by the Assistant Police Chief Levenger. I did not

5   become aware of that suspension until after this lawsuit was filed. There was no indication

6   that the fact Alcevedo was Hispanic played any role in Officer Conlee losing the property.

7

8   I first became aware of Officers Conlee's and Parsell's stop of Mr. Stucky when I received a

9   call from a Nita State Police Sergeant indicating that one of my officers had just stopped a

10   state police officer. The Sergeant did not mention race being a basis for the stop, and did

11   not complain about the stop. I said that I would talk to my officers to find out what hap-

12   pened. I asked the dispatcher to radio Officer Conlee's car and ask him and Officer Parsell

13   to see me when they returned to the station.

14

15   I met with Officers Conlee and Parsell when they came back into the office. I asked them

16   whether they were aware that the person they stopped was a state trooper. They said they

17   were not aware of it at the time of the stop. Officer Conlee stated that he would not even

18   have given Mr. Stucky a warning if he showed them his badge. I was not pleased to hear

19   that from Officer Conlee because we have a regulation in the Policy Manual barring our of-

20   ficers from showing their badge to get favored treatment if they are stopped. Section 3.05

21   states, "An officer shall not use or permit the use of his or her badge in any manner wherein

22   it can reasonably be construed that the officer desires preferential treatment." My position

23   is that if you make a stop you should take some action; either write a citation or a warning.

24

25   I told Officers Conlee and Parsell that I have never asked anyone to void a citation and

26   was not going to start now, that it would be up to them to decide how to proceed. I asked

27   Officer Conlee how he felt about having issued the citation. He was adamant that he had

28   properly written Mr. Stucky up for driving at an unsafe speed because of excessive speed

29   combined with the wet road from the rainy conditions. Officer Conlee told me that he was

30   driving in the left lane when Mr. Stucky's car went flying by him in the right lane, and that

1 he told Officer Parsell, "There is an example of driving at an unsafe speed," because it was

2 raining that day. Officer Conlee said he turned the overhead lights on and Mr. Stucky im-

3 mediately pulled over in front of him. That's the story Officer Conlee related to me. I asked

4 whether either of them had seen who was driving, and both said that they did not because

5 the car went past them so fast. I asked whether Officer Conlee wanted to proceed with the

6 citation, and he said in no uncertain terms that he was following through on the citation

7 that he wrote.

8

9 Officer Conlee told me that Mr. Stucky was very rude and disrespectful when Officer

10 Conlee came up to the car, ignoring Officer Conlee and making calls on his cell phone.

11 Officer Conlee stated that he had never been so disrespected, not only by a police officer,

12 but by anybody in his entire career as a police officer. Officer Conlee indicated that he

13 developed objective suspicion that Mr. Stucky may have been transporting drugs, which

14 is why he sought consent to search.

15

16 After this lawsuit was filed, I asked Officers Conlee and Parsell whether they were aware

17 that Mr. Stucky was black when they made the stop. Officer Conlee indicated he was not

18 aware that Mr. Stucky was African-American until he walked up to Mr. Stucky's car after

19 the stop was made. Officer Parsell told me the exact same thing. If Officers Conlee and

20 Parsell had used Mr. Stucky's race as a basis for the stop, I would have fired them on the

21 spot. Every police officer who works for me knows they would be fired if they used race

22 or ethnicity as a basis for a stop.

23

24 In the years I was investigating crimes, if a suspect told me one story on one occasion

25 and then changed that story, my suspicion of that person increased. If one of my police

26 officers gave one version on a particular occasion and then changed that story, that would

27 increase my suspicion of that officer.

28

29 I made two public statements to reporters once this lawsuit was filed. One of the state-

30 ments was, "The charges are bullshit." I probably should have said "nonsense," but I was

1   angry because Mr. Stucky's allegations are so bogus and outrageous. The most outra-

2   geous thing I've ever encountered in all my life. My second statement was, "I have been

3   around law enforcement for forty years and I have never seen racial profiling. I am really

4   sick of hearing about racial profiling crap." I made these statements because there has

5   been so much publicity about racial profiling, with everyone assuming the officer did

6   something wrong whenever an encounter with an African-American turns violent. As we

7   know from the recent shootings in Dallas and Baton Rouge, being a police officer is a dan-

8   gerous job. My view is that "All Lives Matter," including those of the police. I knew in my

9   heart of hearts that my officers would not do such a thing, and that is why I said I'm tired

10   of this crap, this is wrong.

I have read this deposition, and the answers are true to the best of my knowledge and belief.

/s/Kurt Lieber
Kurt Lieber
Date: July 29, YR-1

/s/Sherry Miller
Sherry Miller
Notary Public

Expert Reports

THOMAS A. GOFORTH
5667 South Green Drive
San Antonio, TX 23156

Attorney Sharon K. Coby
ACLU
105 North Front Street, Suite 225
Nita City, Nita 09101

January 2, YR-0

Attorney Coby:

You provided me with the following documents for review in the case of *Stucky v. Conlee et al.*:

1) Complaint;

2) Answer;

3) Clayton Stucky's deposition transcript;

4) Shelley Elliot's deposition transcript;

5) Nelson Digby's deposition transcript;

6) Officer Conlee and Officer Parsell's deposition transcripts;

7) Chief of Police Lieber's deposition transcript;

8) Transcript of Proceedings before the District Justice;

9) Officer Conlee's past employment reviews as to the category of "lack of prejudice" with the Nita Township Police Department;

10) The City of Nita Police Department's "racial profiling policy" (solely the department's Code of Ethics);

11) Officer Conlee's traffic training document; and

12) City of Nita Police Department Traffic Study.

Following a review of the items forwarded to me in the *Stucky v. Conlee et al.* case, I have the following comments:

In my experience, racial profiling among various law enforcement assignments is indeed real. In short, racial profiling occurs in law enforcement. My opinion results from twenty-eight years of serving in law enforcement; from attending lectures, reading, and research; from discussions with experts who have studied the subject of racial profiling; and lastly, from living in America as an African-American male. The United States Department of Justice Civil Rights Division Investigation of the Ferguson Police Department (DOJ Ferguson Report) in the wake of the shooting of Michael Brown is an excellent primer on bias-based policing. That investigation reveals what evidences biased-based policing; the harmful effects of profiling on not only the victim, but also on the ability of police to safely and effectively do their jobs; and the policies and procedures that should be in place to prevent, address, and remedy instances of discriminatory police action.

Racial profiling is an ineffective and inefficient strategy for policing. As explained in the DOJ Ferguson Report, both research studies and police experience demonstrate that discriminatory police conduct undermines the legitimacy of the police not only in the eyes of the victim, but also for those who observe the conduct. This loss of legitimacy, in turn, increases resistance to enforcement efforts and deters citizens from cooperating with law enforcement officials seeking to prevent and investigate crime. As a result, policing is not only less effective or more difficult, but is less safe for the officers. It is significant that the DOJ Ferguson Report noted that while ensuring officers act in accordance with the Constitution is necessary to improve community trust and public effectiveness, it is not sufficient to do so. In addition to adopting policies and procedures to directly address and redress bias-based policing, the NITA City Police Chief must ensure that his officers treat people respectfully—unlike Officer Conlee's conduct in this case as reported both by Trooper Stucky and Ms. Elliot.

Racial profiling can be both emotionally and physically harmful to the victims of the practice. As the DOJ Ferguson Report astutely observed, "[e]ven relatively routine misconduct . . . can have significant consequences for the people whose rights are violated." That harm can range from depression—caused by the feeling of helplessness that arises when a person is subjected to an unfounded and humiliating search—to the many deaths of unarmed citizens whom the police regarded as so threatening that they shot and killed them. Even people who have not themselves been victims of racial profiling can suffer the loss of a sense of safety. When 911 calls result in the police shooting the person who made the call—which has happened a number of times—then people who need police or emergency services might not call out of fear that their call could result in tragedy. To put it bluntly, people of color are tolerating crimes against themselves because they are more afraid of the police than they are of the criminals. Even an experienced law enforcement officer like Trooper Stucky suffered both personally and professionally from a routine traffic stop.

This loss of trust has larger implications. Profiling harms the relationship between the practicing agency and the community it is serving, not just in emergency situations as mentioned above but in the day-to-day functioning of the community. Policing should not be solely about responding to 911 calls and writing tickets. The police should be a positive presence in the daily life of the community, helping business owners and residents to feel safe and connected to their neighborhood. Children should feel that an officer is someone they can trust. Instead, nonwhite children are continually warned to avoid all contact with the police, because their parents fear that they will be killed. The innocent act of obeying a police command for identification has resulted in more than one shooting when a black man reached for his wallet and the officer assumed that he was going for a gun.

Addressing racial profiling in police and other community agencies can be tricky, because racial profiling is often a product of underlying bias rather than overt prejudice. Many individuals and agencies accused or proven to practice racial profiling defended themselves with aggressive denial of any personal prejudice or acts of racism. I see this defense as a clear lack of understanding about the strategy of racial profiling. Many people in law enforcement have been trained, taught, or conditioned to racially profile as a way to be more effective and efficient—they just don't call it racial profiling. For example, suppose an agency is trained in a strategy commonly known as "Operation Pipeline"—a method of identifying certain roadways as "drug corridors" and targeting stop-and-search efforts in those roadways—and other members of that agency or surrounding agencies see members succeeding with this strategy. The other members or agencies may decide to implement the program, but lose the key questions and identifying patterns that made the original operation successful in targeting drug transporters—without realizing it, these agencies have turned a targeted approach into general racial profiling.

For the most part, the officers in question are not aware that they are profiling. Often they are using the strategy in an effort to protect people and improve public safety. If the agency and/or the community rewards members who implement racial profiling strategies, then we should expect members to continue implementing racial profiling strategies. So pervasive is this pattern that the data often uncovers minority members of an organization using racial profiling strategies against other minority members of a community. A finding such as this does not mean that minority members of the organization are prejudiced; it may simply mean that racial profiling can be a product of underlying bias. The bias being that this strategy, racial profiling, is the way to be successful or rewarded within the organization.

Much of the focus of racial profiling has been on routine traffic stops conducted by the police. The practice of criminal profiling evolved into racial profiling and the terms "driving while black" or "driving while brown" became common ways to explain what minorities experienced and what civil rights activists were attempting to stop. Traffic stops became a focus of concern because most police agencies deploy a large portion of the workforce in patrol cars and give organizational rewards to officers with high numbers of contacts and arrests. As a result, an officer with numerous small or low-level drug arrests is often better rewarded than an officer or agent with one large arrest resulting from an investigation over a two-year period. These rewards are not always blatant. For example, the officer with numerous small or low-level drug arrests may earn overtime for appearing in court four or five times in a two-week pay period. In addition, the higher numbers may also result in nominations as employee of the quarter, building the officer's resume and making him eligible for bonuses or promotions. An officer or agent working a large case targeting an upper-level dealer may have no overtime court cases, and no nominations as employee of the quarter. Plus, once arrests are made in such a large case, the case is generally so solid that a plea agreement is reached and the employee will see no overtime.

Traffic stops are one of the most widespread and visible of police actions. A review of the case studies of turnpike stops in New Jersey and highway stops in Maryland clearly demonstrates that racial profiling occurs in routine traffic stops. Traffic stops are particularly used as a means of procuring the driver's consent to search the vehicle when the officer has a "hunch" about the passengers, but lacks objective reasonable suspicion or probable cause to search the vehicle for contraband.

The DOJ Ferguson Report found that African-Americans were not only disproportionately likely to be subjected to a traffic stop; they were more than twice as likely to be searched during the stop, even though they were found in possession of contraband 26 percent less often than white drivers. Perhaps the most analogous finding of the DOJ Ferguson Report is that not only were African-Americans disproportionately subjected to speeding charges; the disparate impact was 48 percent larger when citations were issued based on the officer's visual assessment rather than electronic speed detection devices. Officers Conlee's and Parsell's stop of Trooper Stucky is a "profile" of racial profiling—a visually based, speed-related stop of an African-American driving a luxury car, followed by a request for consent to search the car.

Racial profiling of this kind is not limited to vehicle stops. A review of "foot stops" by the New York City Police Department also yielded numbers that demonstrated racial profiling. Even in predominantly white neighborhoods, three-quarters or more of the foot stops were of blacks and Latinos. Overall numbers throughout the city showed that black and Latino persons made up almost 90 percent of all stop-and-frisks, with a resulting arrest rate of less than 2 percent. The stop-and-frisk program did very little to curb crime, but fostered a huge distrust and fear of the police.

This points to another very real problem with racial profiling: the issue of perception. When an agency fails to maintain data about incidence reports or the feedback received from citizens, or fails to provide training, or to have a stated policy addressing racial profiling, then the perception that the agency engages in racial profiling becomes a serious problem. Policing is very dependent on public trust; the police and the community must work together. When an agency's response to profiling allegations and community feedback is a series of stonewalling comments—"We do not do it," or "I have never seen it"—that agency has failed to respond to the concerns of the community. Such a failure erodes the relationship between the community and the agency, and leads to a cycle of alienation.

Despite the evidence demonstrating these problems with racial profiling, there are still individuals and groups who support profiling in the name of effectiveness and efficiency. And when you are look at raw statistics, some of their arguments can seem convincing: the raw statistics consistently show that racial minorities account for a majority of arrests, convictions, and prison populations. These raw statistics fail, however, to take into consideration the fact that minority felons receive consistently harsher sentences for the same crimes committed by Caucasians, or that Caucasians are charged with lesser offenses for the same criminal activity. They do not account for the number of Caucasians who are let off with a warning, which is anecdotally much higher than the number of persons of color who only receive warnings at a stop. Statistics show that, when a vehicle is searched at a traffic stop, Caucasians are much more likely to be found carrying contraband items than persons of color. But Caucasians are stopped for searches at a far lower rate than persons of color.

This brings us to the stop, and subsequent search, of Clayton Stucky's vehicle. My job in this matter is not to make a determination of the legal soundness of the officers' decision to stop Trooper Stucky, but to review the underlying profiling policy of the police department. In my opinion, the Nita City Police Department suffers from a severe lack of awareness and monitoring of racial profiling issues. The department needs to develop strategies to monitor allegations of racial profiling, and these strategies need to be documented and shared with the community.

Chief Lieber's deliberate indifference to racial profiling is demonstrated by his lack of policy on the matter. The issue of racial profiling has been the subject of books, training seminars, conferences, case law, movies, and even television shows since the early 1990s. Yet he has no specific policy specifically banning racial profiling. Chief Lieber needs to ensure that his employees have clear and specific guidance with regards to racial profiling. The department's Law Enforcement Code of Ethics fails as an adequate policy for racial profiling. Chief Lieber's failure to promulgate a specific racial profiling policy demonstrates deliberate indifference to the risk of racial profiling. His claim that he has "never seen it" does not justify the lack of a specific policy on the issue. Perhaps the chief has never shot anyone during the course of his duties, and maybe he has never been present when someone else in law enforcement shot someone. Yet the chief knows that his deputies need policies in the use of deadly force.

The absence of any policy explicitly prohibiting racial profiling or bias-based policing is exacerbated by Chief Lieber's failure to provide any training to reduce the impact of bias in policing. The DOJ Ferguson Report specifically recommended "initial and recurring training to all officers that sends a clear, consistent and emphatic message that bias-based profiling and other forms of discriminatory policing are prohibited." The Report recommends that training extend to supervisors and commanders to facilitate their ability to detect and respond to profiling. Lorie Friedell, an associate professor of criminology at the University of South Florida who received Department of Justice funds to develop the training program called Fair and Impartial Policing, warned that traditional diversity or sensitivity training is inadequate because it fails to address implicit bias. See Benedict Carey and Erica Good, *Police Try to Lower Racial Bias, but Under Pressure, It Isn't So Easy*, NEW YORK TIMES, July 11, 2016.

The Nita City Police Department's training on traffic issues also is deliberately indifferent to the risk of racial profiling. This training, designed by Officer Conlee and reviewed by Chief Lieber, ignores the topic of racial profiling. The DOJ Ferguson Report recommends specific measures designed to prevent biased-based policing in traffic stops, including instruction on applicable legal standards for vehicle searches, and a prohibition "for the foreseeable future" of searches based on consent. The DOJ further recommends that training go beyond Fourth Amendment standards to address the responsibility of officers to constrain action beyond constitutional boundaries in order to promote public safety and community trust.

Chief Lieber's lack of statistics gathering in the area of traffic data and search data further demonstrates deliberate disregard of the risk of racial profiling. The chief claims that his officers do not engage in racial profiling, but yet he has no data or evidence to support this position. The after-the-fact traffic study is flawed in many ways. Use of the driver's license photo to determine the race of drivers who have been stopped is not a reliable way to determine their actual race. The census data used in the study does not reliably document the percentage of persons of each race who are licensed drivers in the City or County of Nita; nor does that data reflect the number of drivers who may live outside the City and County of Nita but may regularly drive in the city limits for business or personal reasons. Finally, the traffic study does not reflect drivers who were stopped but were not issued written warnings or citations. An officer who makes a traffic stop on the basis of race, procures consent to search, but finds no contraband in the vehicle often will not issue a warning or citation in order to minimize the incentive for the driver to sue to contest the stop.

Chief Lieber further demonstrated indifference through his lack of any citizen complaint procedure. The DOJ Ferguson Report noted that preventing police misconduct, building community confidence, and establishing police legitimacy require formal mechanisms for accepting, investigating and responding to complaints of misconduct. While fundamentally flawed in its operation, Ferguson at least had a formal process for receipt of complaints. Interestingly, one of the defects in the operation of the Ferguson process was that the Police Department frequently assumed the officer is telling the truth, accepting the word of the officer over the complainant. Chief Lieber manifested the same pathology, accepting Officers Conlee and Parsell's version of the events. As Chief Lieber stated in his deposition, he never has ordered an officer to withdraw charges over the officer's objection. The Ferguson complaint procedure was further infected by the failure to sanction officers who lie in the course of an investigation of a complaint. In addition to accepting his officers' recounting of the traffic stop, the record indicates that Chief Lieber took no action in response to the fact that Officer Parsell falsely advised Chief Lieber that Officer Parsell did not know Trooper Stucky was African-American until he approached Trooper Stucky's car after it was stopped. Officer Parsell's deposition, under oath, plainly demonstrated that he was fully aware that Trooper Stucky was a person of color before they activated the overhead lights in the police car.

Chief Lieber's failure to provide any policy or training squarely addressing bias-based policing, combined with the absence of any effective means for citizens to complain about being racially profiled, made it inevitable that Nita City Police Department officers would use race in traffic stops. The confidence of Nita City Police that they could reap the perceived rewards of bias-based policing free from adverse consequences was bolstered by the lack of sufficient scrutiny in the hiring process and lack of formal evaluation once on the job. The DOJ Ferguson report recommended that in the case of lateral hires, the department should scrutinize the record of the employee. When hiring Officer Conlee, Chief Lieber never obtained Officer Conlee's performance evaluations from Nita Township. The evaluations in the category of "lack of prejudice" indicated that Officer Conlee did not always act in a colorblind manner. Chief Lieber also made no further inquiry in response to Chief Ellis' admonition not to make Officer Conlee a supervisor. Whatever abuses of Officer Conlee's supervisory duties gave rise to Chief Ellis's warning may well have manifested themselves in his supervision of Officer Parsell, leaving Officer Parsell no choice but to be complicit in the conduct and aftermath of the stop of Trooper Stucky.

It is not uncommon for a police chief to state that he has never seen racial profiling. This individual may be detached from the day-to-day actions of the street officer. Even if a chief engages in the occasional ride-along, it is highly unlikely that the officer is going to say, "I am going to stop this car because of the color of the driver's skin." If the chief actually engaged in racial profiling during his or her time in patrol, it is likely they had a pretext for the stop and never considered their action to be racial profiling. As a result, if the chief felt defensive, he may indeed say he has never seen it, so it must not exist. This type of response does not acknowledge that at some point in history, in some communities, racial profiling may have been taught, trained, expected, and rewarded. For example, when I was selling books door to door in the community of Mobile, Alabama during the late 1960s I mistakenly ventured into a white neighborhood. Within minutes I was confronted by the police, detained, and questioned. The police explained that I could sell my books, but I was to stay out of certain neighborhoods in Mobile. The police officers were simply explaining the expectations according to the people and leadership in Mobile. I have no evidence that they themselves were racist, but the policy certainly was. In short, I am disappointed that the chief's response was, "I have never seen it," but I am not surprised. The chief does not understand that racial profiling can still be real, even if he has never seen racial profiling.

Far more illuminating is his public proclamation that Trooper Stucky's charges were "bullshit" and that Chief Lieber was "tired of hearing about racial profiling crap." These comments are akin to the view of City of Ferguson officials that the disparate law enforcement contact with persons of color was due to a pervasive lack of "personal responsibility" among certain segments of the community. The DOJ Ferguson Report properly found this reaction to reflect racial stereotyping that supported the finding of intentional discrimination.

The issue of Officer Conlee being a training officer goes beyond the discipline within the Police Department. I can see how the chief saw Officer Conlee's discipline matters as a jail and transport issue, not a traffic issue. For example, an officer who writes poor incident reports and presents a poor appearance in court may indeed make an excellent firearms instructor because he knows the mechanics of shooting. I think the chief should have had more focus on the prior performance evaluations of Officer Conlee before making him a trainer. Chief Ellis told Chief Lieber not to make Officer Conlee a supervisor. And the evaluations in the category of "lack of prejudice" also indicated that Officer Conlee did not always act in a colorblind manner. I think Chief Lieber needs to pay additional attention to detail. But I cannot say that the discipline alone would be reason to remove Officer Conlee from his trainer status.

The totality of Chief Lieber's lack of policy, training, and monitoring of actions by his officers indicates deliberate indifference to the risk of racial profiling. The provided documents show no effort on the part of the chief to address the topic or any resulting issues arising from racial profiling. The chief claims to run a professional organization where everyone knows his expectations. Yet Officer Conlee was disciplined for not following property procedures and the chief was not made aware of the matter. Chief Lieber never set any expectations with regards to the matter of racial profiling. If Chief Lieber had gotten the organization accredited or at least had his policies reviewed by the National or the International Association of Chiefs of Police, then he may have been informed about racial profiling or his lack of policy. But by not reaching out for any type of peer review, by not staying abreast of modern police practices, and by authorizing traffic enforcement training that did not address the issue of profiling, Chief Lieber has been deliberately indifferent to the risk of racial profiling.

When an agency fails to provide any data, feedback, training, or policy around the issue of racial profiling, then it is much more likely that perception of profiling becomes real. Policing is very dependent on public trust and the police and the community must work together. When the agency feedback is a series of comments like, "We do not do it," or "I have never seen it," the agency has failed to respond to the needs of the community. The City of Nita Police Department needs to look for ways to monitor the risk of racial profiling and these strategies need to be documented and shared with the community. Strategies could include 1) detailed and valid traffic stop data that is shared with the public; 2) detailed arrest data; 3) detailed complaint data; 4) an internal affairs system; 5) an anti-racial profiling policy; and 6) anti-racial profiling training provided by an outside vendor.

I attach an extensive excerpt from the Ferguson report to this letter. I have not given any expert testimony in the last four years. In prior expert testimony agreements I have quoted $150.00 per hour as a review rate and $250.00 per hour as a testimony rate. I do not know if my consultant contract with ACLU allows for this additional payment.

Sincerely,

/s/ *Thomas A. Goforth*
Thomas A. Goforth, PhD

VERIFICATION PURSUANT TO 28 U.S.C.A. § 1746

I, Thomas A. Goforth, PhD, declare under penalty of perjury that the facts contained within the foregoing Expert Report are true and correct to the best of my knowledge.

/s/ *Thomas A. Goforth*
Thomas A. Goforth, PhD

Investigation of the Ferguson Police Department

United States Department of Justice Civil Rights Division

March 4, 2015

[Excerpted. Full report available at http://bit.ly/1lV31kb]

REPORT SUMMARY

The Civil Rights Division of the United States Department of Justice opened its investigation of the Ferguson Police Department ("FPD") on September 4, 2014. This investigation was initiated under the pattern-or-practice provision of the Violent Crime Control and Law Enforcement Act of 1994, 42 U.S.C. § 14141, the Omnibus Crime Control and Safe Streets Act of 1968, 42 U.S.C. § 3789d ("Safe Streets Act"), and Title VI of the Civil Rights Act of 1964, 42 U.S.C. § 2000d ("Title VI"). This investigation has revealed a pattern or practice of unlawful conduct within the Ferguson Police Department that violates the First, Fourth, and Fourteenth Amendments to the United States Constitution, and federal statutory law.

Over the course of the investigation, we interviewed City officials, including City Manager John Shaw, Mayor James Knowles, Chief of Police Thomas Jackson, Municipal Judge Ronald Brockmeyer, the Municipal Court Clerk, Ferguson's Finance Director, half of FPD's sworn officers, and others. We spent, collectively, approximately 100 person-days onsite in Ferguson. We participated in ride-alongs with on-duty officers, reviewed over 35,000 pages of police records as well as thousands of emails and other electronic materials provided by the police department. Enlisting the assistance of statistical experts, we analyzed FPD's data on stops, searches, citations, and arrests, as well as data collected by the municipal court. We observed four separate sessions of Ferguson Municipal Court, interviewing dozens of people charged with local offenses, and we reviewed third-party studies regarding municipal court practices in Ferguson and St. Louis County more broadly. As in all of our investigations, we sought to engage the local community, conducting hundreds of in-person and telephone interviews of individuals who reside in Ferguson or who have had interactions with the police department. We contacted ten neighborhood associations and met with each group that responded to us, as well as several other community groups and advocacy organizations.

Throughout the investigation, we relied on two police chiefs who accompanied us to Ferguson and who themselves interviewed City and police officials, spoke with community members, and reviewed FPD policies and incident reports.

* * * * *

Ferguson's law enforcement practices are shaped by the City's focus on revenue rather than by public safety needs. This emphasis on revenue has compromised the institutional character of Ferguson's police department, contributing to a pattern of unconstitutional policing, and has also shaped its municipal court, leading to procedures that raise due process concerns and inflict unnecessary harm on members of the Ferguson community. Further, Ferguson's police and municipal court practices both reflect and exacerbate existing racial bias, including racial stereotypes. Ferguson's own data establish clear racial disparities that adversely impact African Americans. The evidence shows that discriminatory intent is part of the reason for these disparities. Over time, Ferguson's police and municipal court practices have sown deep mistrust between parts of the community and the police department, undermining law enforcement legitimacy among African Americans in particular.

Focus on Generating Revenue

The City budgets for sizeable increases in municipal fines and fees each year, exhorts police and court staff to deliver those revenue increases, and closely monitors whether those increases are achieved. City officials routinely urge Chief Jackson to generate more revenue through enforcement. . . . Ferguson police officers from all ranks told us that revenue generation is stressed heavily within the police department, and that the message comes from City leadership. The evidence we reviewed supports this perception.

Police Practices

The City's emphasis on revenue generation has a profound effect on FPD's approach to law enforcement. Patrol assignments and schedules are geared toward aggressive enforcement of Ferguson's municipal code, with insufficient thought given to whether enforcement strategies promote public safety or unnecessarily undermine community trust and cooperation. Officer evaluations and promotions depend to an inordinate degree on "productivity," meaning the number of citations issued. Partly as a consequence of City and FPD priorities, many officers appear to see some residents, especially those who live in Ferguson's predominantly African-American neighborhoods, less as constituents to be protected than as potential offenders and sources of revenue.

. . . Police supervisors and leadership do too little to ensure that officers act in accordance with law and policy, and rarely respond meaningfully to civilian complaints of officer misconduct. The result is a pattern of stops without reasonable suspicion and arrests without probable cause in violation of the Fourth Amendment; infringement on free expression, as well as retaliation for protected expression, in violation of the First Amendment; and excessive force in violation of the Fourth Amendment.

Even relatively routine misconduct by Ferguson police officers can have significant consequences for the people whose rights are violated. . . .

Municipal Court Practices

Ferguson has allowed its focus on revenue generation to fundamentally compromise the role of Ferguson's municipal court. The municipal court does not act as a neutral arbiter of the law or a check on unlawful police conduct. Instead, the court primarily uses its judicial authority as the means to compel the payment of fines and fees that advance the City's financial interests. This has led to court practices that violate the Fourteenth Amendment's due process and equal protection requirements. The court's practices also impose unnecessary harm, overwhelmingly on African-American individuals, and run counter to public safety.

* * * * *

Together, these court practices exacerbate the harm of Ferguson's unconstitutional police practices. They impose a particular hardship upon Ferguson's most vulnerable residents, especially upon those living in or near poverty. Minor offenses can generate crippling debts, result in jail time because of an inability to pay, and result in the loss of a driver's license, employment, or housing.

* * * * *

<u>Racial Bias</u>

Ferguson's approach to law enforcement both reflects and reinforces racial bias, including stereotyping. The harms of Ferguson's police and court practices are borne disproportionately by African Americans, and there is evidence that this is due in part to intentional discrimination on the basis of race.

Ferguson's law enforcement practices overwhelmingly impact African Americans. Data collected by the Ferguson Police Department from 2012 to 2014 shows that African Americans account for 85% of vehicle stops, 90% of citations, and 93% of arrests made by FPD officers, despite comprising only 67% of Ferguson's population. African Americans are more than twice as likely as white drivers to be searched during vehicle stops even after controlling for non-race based variables such as the reason the vehicle stop was initiated, but are found in possession of contraband 26% less often than white drivers, suggesting officers are impermissibly considering race as a factor when determining whether to search. African Americans are more likely to be cited and arrested following a stop regardless of why the stop was initiated and are more likely to receive multiple citations during a single incident. . . . Notably, with respect to speeding charges brought by FPD, the evidence shows not only that African Americans are represented at disproportionately high rates overall, but also that the disparate impact of FPD's enforcement practices on African Americans is 48% larger when citations are issued not on the basis of radar or laser, but by some other method, such as the officer's own visual assessment.

These disparities are also present in FPD's use of force. Nearly 90% of documented force used by FPD officers was used against African Americans. In every canine bite incident for which racial information is available, the person bitten was African American.

* * * * *

Our investigation indicates that this disproportionate burden on African Americans cannot be explained by any difference in the rate at which people of different races violate the law. Rather, our investigation has revealed that these disparities occur, at least in part, because of unlawful bias against and stereotypes about African Americans. We have found substantial evidence of racial bias among police and court staff in Ferguson. For example, we discovered emails circulated by police supervisors and court staff that stereotype racial minorities as criminals, including one email that joked about an abortion by an African-American woman being a means of crime control.

City officials have frequently asserted that the harsh and disparate results of Ferguson's law enforcement system do not indicate problems with police or court practices, but instead reflect a pervasive lack of "personal responsibility" among "certain segments" of the community.

Our investigation has found that the practices about which area residents have complained are in fact unconstitutional and unduly harsh. But the City's personal-responsibility refrain is telling: it reflects many of the same racial stereotypes found in the emails between police and court supervisors. This evidence of bias and stereotyping, together with evidence that Ferguson has long recognized but failed to correct the consistent racial disparities caused by its police and court practices, demonstrates that the discriminatory effects of Ferguson's conduct are driven at least in part by discriminatory intent in violation of the Fourteenth Amendment.

* * * * *

II.   BACKGROUND

The City of Ferguson is one of 89 municipalities in St. Louis County, Missouri. According to United States Census Data from 2010, Ferguson is home to roughly 21,000 residents. While Ferguson's total population has stayed relatively constant in recent decades, Ferguson's racial demographics have changed dramatically during that time. In 1990, 74% of Ferguson's population was white, while 25% was black. By 2000, African Americans became the new majority, making up 52% of the City's population. According to the 2010 Census, the black population in Ferguson has grown to 67%, whereas the white population has decreased to 29%. According to the 2009-2013 American Community Survey, 25% of the City's population lives below the federal poverty level.

* * * * *

IV.   FERGUSON LAW ENFORCEMENT PRACTICES VIOLATE THE LAW AND UNDERMINE COMMUNITY TRUST, ESPECIALLY AMONG AFRICAN AMERICANS

* * * * *

1.   FPD Engages in a Pattern of Unconstitutional Stops and Arrests in Violation of the Fourth Amendment

FPD's approach to law enforcement has led officers to conduct stops and arrests that violate the Constitution. We identified several elements to this pattern of misconduct. Frequently, officers stop people without reasonable suspicion or arrest them without probable cause. . . . The data show, moreover, that FPD misconduct in the area of stops and arrests disproportionately impacts African Americans.

* * * * *

C. Ferguson Law Enforcement Practices Disproportionately Harm Ferguson's African-American Residents and Are Driven in Part by Racial Bias

Ferguson's police and municipal court practices disproportionately harm African Americans. Further, our investigation found substantial evidence that this harm stems in part from intentional discrimination in violation of the Constitution.

African Americans experience disparate impact in nearly every aspect of Ferguson's law enforcement system. Despite making up 67% of the population, African Americans accounted for 85% of FPD's traffic stops, 90% of FPD's citations, and 93% of FPD's arrests from 2012 to 2014. Other statistical disparities, set forth in detail below, show that in Ferguson:

- African Americans are 2.07 times more likely to be searched during a vehicular stop but are 26% less likely to have contraband found on them during a search. They are 2.00 times more likely to receive a citation and 2.37 times more likely to be arrested following a vehicular stop.

- African Americans have force used against them at disproportionately high rates, accounting for 88% of all cases from 2010 to August 2014 in which an FPD officer reported using force. In all 14 uses of force involving a canine bite for which we have information about the race of the person bitten, the person was African American.

- African Americans are more likely to receive multiple citations during a single incident, receiving four or more citations on 73 occasions between October 2012 and July 2014, whereas non-African Americans received four or more citations only twice during that period.

- African Americans account for 95% of Manner of Walking charges; 94% of all Fail to Comply charges; 92% of all Resisting Arrest charges; 92% of all Peace Disturbance charges; and 89% of all Failure to Obey charges.[1]

- African Americans are 68% less likely than others to have their cases dismissed by the Municipal Judge, and in 2013 African Americans accounted for 92% of cases in which an arrest warrant was issued.

- African Americans account for 96% of known arrests made exclusively because of an outstanding municipal warrant.

These disparities are not the necessary or unavoidable results of legitimate public safety efforts. In fact, the practices that lead to these disparities in many ways undermine law enforcement effectiveness. *See, e.g.*, Jack Glaser, *Suspect Race: Causes and Consequence of Racial Profiling* 96-126 (2015) (because profiling can increase crime while harming communities, it has a "high risk" of contravening the core police objectives of controlling crime and promoting public safety). The disparate impact of these practices thus violates federal law, including Title VI and the Safe Streets Act.

---

1 As noted above, FPD charges violations of Municipal Code Section 29-16 as both Failure to Obey and Failure to Comply. Court data carries forward this inconsistency.

The racially disparate impact of Ferguson's practices is driven, at least in part, by intentional discrimination in violation of the Equal Protection Clause of the Fourteenth Amendment. Racial bias and stereotyping is evident from the facts, taken together. This evidence includes: the consistency and magnitude of the racial disparities throughout Ferguson's police and court enforcement actions; the selection and execution of police and court practices that disproportionately harm African Americans and do little to promote public safety; the persistent exercise of discretion to the detriment of African Americans; the apparent consideration of race in assessing threat; and the historical opposition to having African Americans live in Ferguson, which lingers among some today. We have also found explicit racial bias in the communications of police and court supervisors and that some officials apply racial stereotypes, rather than facts, to explain the harm African Americans experience due to Ferguson's approach to law enforcement. "Determining whether invidious discriminatory purpose was a motivating factor demands a sensitive inquiry into such circumstantial and direct evidence of intent as may be available." *Vill. of Arlington Heights v. Metro. Hous. Dev. Corp.*, 429 U.S. 252, 266 (1977). Based on this evidence as a whole, we have found that Ferguson's law enforcement activities stem in part from a discriminatory purpose and thus deny African Americans equal protection of the laws in violation of the Constitution.

2. Ferguson's Law Enforcement Actions Impose a Disparate Impact on African Americans that Violates Federal Law

* * * * *

a. Disparate Impact of FPD Practices

    i. *Disparate Impact of FPD Enforcement Actions Arising from Vehicular Stops*

Pursuant to Missouri state law on racial profiling, Mo. Rev. Stat. § 590.650, FPD officers are required to collect race and other data during every traffic stop. While some law enforcement agencies collect more comprehensive data to identify and stem racial profiling, this information is sufficient to show that FPD practices exert a racially disparate impact along several dimensions.

FPD reported 11,610 vehicle stops between October 2012 and October 2014. African Americans accounted for 85%, or 9,875, of those stops, despite making up only 67% of the population. White individuals made up 15%, or 1,735, of stops during that period, despite representing 29% of the population. These differences indicate that FPD traffic stop practices may disparately impact black drivers.[2] Even setting aside the question of whether there are racial disparities in FPD's traffic

---

2 While there are limitations to using basic population data as a benchmark when evaluating whether there are racial disparities in vehicle stops, it is sufficiently reliable here. In fact, in Ferguson, black drivers might account for *less* of the driving pool than would be expected from overall population rates because a lower proportion of blacks than whites is at or above the minimum driving age. *See 2009-2013 5-Year American Community Survey*, U.S. Census Bureau (2015) (showing higher proportion of black population in under-15 and under-19 age categories than white population). Ferguson officials have told us that they believe that black drivers account for *more* of the driving pool than their 67% share of the population because the driving pool also includes drivers traveling from neighboring municipalities—many of which have higher black populations than Ferguson. Our investigation casts doubt upon that claim. An analysis of zip-code data from the 53,850 summonses FPD issued from January 1, 2009 to October 14, 2014, shows that the African-American makeup for all zip codes receiving a summons—weighted by population size and the number of summonses

stop practices, however, the data collected during those stops reliably shows statistically significant racial disparities in the *outcomes* people receive *after* being stopped. Unlike with vehicle stops, assessing the disparate impact of post-stop outcomes—such as the rate at which stops result in citations, searches, or arrests—is not dependent on population data or on assumptions about differential offending rates by race; instead, the enforcement actions imposed against stopped black drivers are compared directly to the enforcement actions imposed against stopped white drivers.

In Ferguson, traffic stops of black drivers are more likely to lead to searches, citations, and arrests than are stops of white drivers. Black people are significantly more likely to be searched during a traffic stop than white people. From October 2012 to October 2014, 11% of stopped black drivers were searched, whereas only 5% of stopped white drivers were searched.

Despite being searched at higher rates, African Americans are 26% *less* likely to have contraband found on them than whites: 24% of searches of African Americans resulted in a contraband finding, whereas 30% of searches of whites resulted in a contraband finding. This disparity exists even after controlling for the type of search conducted, whether a search incident to arrest, a consent search, or a search predicated on reasonable suspicion. The lower rate at which officers find contraband when searching African Americans indicates either that officers' suspicion of criminal wrongdoing is less likely to be accurate when interacting with African Americans or that officers are more likely to search African Americans without any suspicion of criminal wrongdoing. Either explanation suggests bias, whether explicit or implicit.[3] This lower hit rate for African Americans also underscores that this disparate enforcement practice is ineffective.

Other, more subtle indicators likewise show meaningful disparities in FPD's search practices: of the 31 *Terry* stop searches FPD conducted during this period between October 2012 to October 2014, 30 were of black individuals; of the 103 times FPD asked both the driver and passenger to exit a vehicle during a search, the searched individuals were black in 95 cases; and, while only one search of a white person lasted more than half an hour (1% of all searches of white drivers), 59 searches of African Americans lasted that long (5% of all searches of black drivers).

Of all stopped black drivers, 91%, or 8,987, received citations, while 87%, or 1,501, of all stopped white drivers received a citation.[4] 891 stopped black drivers—10% of all stopped black drivers—were arrested as a result of the stop, whereas only 63 stopped white drivers—4% of all stopped white drivers—were arrested. This disparity is explainable in large part by the high number of black individuals arrested for outstanding municipal warrants issued for missed court payments and appearances. As we discuss below, African Americans are more likely to have warrants issued against them than whites and are more likely to be arrested for an outstanding warrant than their

---

received by people from that zip code—is 63%. Thus, there is substantial reason to believe that the share of drivers in Ferguson who are black is in fact *lower* than population data suggests.

3 Assessing contraband or "hit rates" is a generally accepted practice in the field of criminology to "operationaliz[e] the concept of 'intent to discriminate.'" The test shows "bias against a protected group if the success rate of searches on that group is lower than on another group." Nicola Persico & Petra Todd, *The Hit Rates Test for Racial Bias in Motor-Vehicle Searches*, 25 Justice Quarterly 37, 52 (2008). Indeed, as noted below, in assessing whether racially disparate impact is motivated by discriminatory intent for Equal Protection Clause purposes, disparity can itself provide probative evidence of discriminatory intent.

4 As noted above, African Americans received 90% of all citations issued by FPD from October 2012 to July 2014. This data shows that 86% of people receiving citations following an FPD traffic stop between October 2012 and October 2014 were African American.

white counterparts. Notably, on 14 occasions FPD listed the only reason for an arrest following a traffic stop as "resisting arrest." In all 14 of those cases, the person arrested was black.

These disparities in the outcomes that result from traffic stops remain even after regression analysis is used to control for non-race-based variables, including driver age; gender; the assignment of the officer making the stop; disparities in officer behavior; and the stated reason the stop was initiated. Upon accounting for differences in those variables, African Americans remained 2.07 times more likely to be searched; 2.00 times more likely to receive a citation; and 2.37 times more likely to be arrested than other stopped individuals. Each of these disparities is statistically significant and would occur by chance less than one time in 1,000.[5] The odds of these disparities occurring by chance together are significantly lower still.

* * * * *

ii.   *Disparate Impact of Other FPD Charging Practices*

From October 2012 to July 2014, African Americans accounted for 85%, or 30,525, of the 35,871 *total* charges brought by FPD—including traffic citations, summonses, and arrests. Non-African Americans accounted for 15%, or 5,346, of all charges brought during that period. These rates vary somewhat across different offenses. For example, African Americans represent a relatively low proportion of those charged with Driving While Intoxicated and Speeding on State Roads or Highways. With respect to speeding offenses for all roads, African Americans account for 72% of citations based on radar or laser, but 80% of citations based on other or unspecified methods. Thus, as evaluated by radar, African Americans violate the law at lower rates than as evaluated by FPD officers. Indeed, controlling for other factors, the disparity in speeding tickets between African Americans and non-African Americans is 48% larger when citations are issued not on the basis of radar or laser, but by some other method, such as the officer's own visual assessment. This difference is statistically significant.

* * * * *

3.   Ferguson's Law Enforcement Practices Are Motivated in Part by Discriminatory Intent in Violation of the Fourteenth Amendment and Other Federal Laws

The race-based disparities created by Ferguson's law enforcement practices cannot be explained by chance or by any difference in the rates at which people of different races adhere to the law. These disparities occur, at least in part, because Ferguson law enforcement practices are directly shaped and perpetuated by racial bias. Those practices thus operate in violation of the Fourteenth Amendment's Equal Protection Clause, which prohibits discriminatory policing on the

---

5 It is generally accepted practice in the field of statistics to consider any result that would occur by chance less than five times out of 100 to be statistically significant.

basis of race. *Whren* [*v. United States*, 517 U.S. 806] at 813 [(1996)]; *Johnson v. Crooks*, 326 F.3d 995, 999 (8th Cir. 2003).

* * * * *

a.   Consistency and Magnitude of Identified Racial Disparities

In assessing whether an official action was motivated in part by discriminatory intent, the actual impact of the action and whether it "bears more heavily on one race or another" may "provide an important starting point." *Vill. of Arlington Heights*, 429 U.S. at 266 (internal citations and quotation marks omitted). Indeed, in rare cases, statistical evidence of discriminatory impact may be sufficiently probative to itself establish discriminatory intent. *Hazelwood School Dist. v. United States*, 433 U.S. 299, 307-08 (1977) (noting in the Title VII context that where "gross statistical disparities can be shown, they alone may in a proper case constitute prima facie proof of a pattern or practice of discrimination").

The race-based disparities we have found are not isolated or aberrational; rather, they exist in nearly every aspect of Ferguson police and court operations. As discussed above, statistical analysis shows that African Americans are more likely to be searched but less likely to have contraband found on them; more likely to receive a citation following a stop and more likely to receive multiple citations at once; more likely to be arrested; more likely to have force used against them; more likely to have their case last longer and require more encounters with the municipal court; more likely to have an arrest warrant issued against them by the municipal court; and more likely to be arrested solely on the basis of an outstanding warrant. As noted above, many of these disparities would occur by chance less than one time in 1000.

These disparities provide significant evidence of discriminatory intent, as the "impact of an official action is often probative of why the action was taken in the first place since people usually intend the natural consequences of their actions." *Reno v. Bossier Parish Sch. Bd.*, 520 U.S. 471, 487 (1997); *see also Davis*, 426 U.S. at 242 ("An invidious discriminatory purpose may often be inferred from the totality of the relevant facts, including the fact, if it is true, that the [practice] bears more heavily on one race than another."). These disparities are unexplainable on grounds other than race and evidence that racial bias, whether implicit or explicit, has shaped law enforcement conduct.[6]

b.   Direct Evidence of Racial Bias

Our investigation uncovered direct evidence of racial bias in the communications of influential Ferguson decision makers. In email messages and during interviews, several court and law enforcement personnel expressed discriminatory views and intolerance with regard to race, religion,

---

6 Social psychologists have long recognized the influence of implicit racial bias on decision making, and law enforcement experts have similarly acknowledged the impact of implicit racial bias on law enforcement decisions. *See, e.g.*, R. Richard Banks, Jennifer L. Eberhardt, & Lee Ross, *Discrimination and Implicit Bias in a Racially Unequal Society*, 94 Cal. L. Rev. 1169 (2006); Tracey G. Gove, *Implicit Bias and Law Enforcement*, The Police Chief (October 2011).

and national origin. The content of these communications is unequivocally derogatory, dehumanizing, and demonstrative of impermissible bias.

* * * * *

This documentary evidence of explicit racial bias is consistent with reports from community members indicating that some FPD officers use racial epithets in dealing with members of the public. . . .

Courts have widely acknowledged that direct statements exhibiting racial bias are exceedingly rare, and that such statements are not necessary for establishing the existence of discriminatory purpose. *See, e.g., Hayden v. Paterson*, 594 F.3d 150, 163 (2d Cir. 2010) (noting that "discriminatory intent is rarely susceptible to direct proof"); *see also Thomas v. Eastman Kodak Co.*, 183 F.3d 38, 64 (1st Cir. 1999) (noting in Title VII case that "[t]here is no requirement that a plaintiff . . . must present direct, 'smoking gun' evidence of racially biased decision making in order to prevail"); *Robinson v. Runyon,* 149 F.3d 507, 513 (6th Cir. 1998) (noting in Title VII case that "[r]arely will there be direct evidence from the lips of the defendant proclaiming his or her racial animus"). Where such evidence does exist, however, it is highly probative of discriminatory intent. That is particularly true where, as here, the communications exhibiting bias are made by those with considerable decision-making authority. *See Doe v. Mamaroneck*, 462 F. Supp. 2d 520, 550 (S.D.N.Y. 2006); *Eberhart v. Gettys*, 215 F. Supp. 2d 666, 678 (M.D.N.C. 2002).

c.　　Evidence of Racial Stereotyping

Several Ferguson officials told us during our investigation that it is a lack of "personal responsibility" among African-American members of the Ferguson community that causes African Americans to experience disproportionate harm under Ferguson's approach to law enforcement. Our investigation suggests that this explanation is at odd with the facts. While there are people of all races who may lack personal responsibility, the harm of Ferguson's approach to law enforcement is largely due to the myriad systemic deficiencies discussed above. Our investigation revealed African Americans making extraordinary efforts to pay off expensive tickets for minor, often unfairly charged, violations, despite systemic obstacles to resolving those tickets. While our investigation did not indicate that African Americans are disproportionately irresponsible, it did reveal that, as the [above-mentioned] emails reflect, some Ferguson decision makers hold negative stereotypes about African Americans, and lack of personal responsibility is one of them. Application of this stereotype furthers the disproportionate impact of Ferguson's police and court practices.

* * * * *

d.　　Historical Background

Until the 1960s, Ferguson was a "sundown town" where African Americans were banned from the City after dark. The City would block off the main road from Kinloch, which was a poor, all-black suburb, "with a chain and construction materials but kept a second road open during the day so housekeepers and nannies could get from Kinloch to jobs in Ferguson."[7] During our investigative interviews, several older African-American residents recalled this era in Ferguson and recounted that African Americans knew that, for them, the City was "off-limits."

The Ferguson of half a century ago is not the same Ferguson that exists today. We heard from many residents—black and white—who expressed pride in their community, especially with regard to the fact that Ferguson is one of the most demographically diverse communities in the area. Pride in this aspect of Ferguson is well founded; Ferguson is more diverse than most of the United States, and than many of its surrounding cities. It is clear that many Ferguson residents of different races genuinely embrace that diversity.

But we also found evidence during our investigation that some within Ferguson still have difficulty coming to terms with Ferguson's changing demographics and seeing Ferguson's African American and white residents as equals in civic life. While total population rates have remained relatively constant over the last three decades, the portion of Ferguson residents who are African American has increased steadily but dramatically, from 25% in 1990 to 67% in 2010. Some individuals, including individuals charged with discretionary enforcement decisions in either the police department or the court, have expressed concerns about the increasing number of African Americans that have moved to Ferguson in recent years. Similarly, some City officials and residents we spoke with explicitly distinguished Ferguson's African-American residents from Ferguson's "normal" residents or "regular" people. One white third-generation Ferguson resident told us that in many ways Ferguson is "progressive and quite vibrant," while in another it is "typical—trying to hang on to its 'whiteness.'"

On its own, Ferguson's historical backdrop as a racially segregated community that did not treat African Americans equally under the law does not demonstrate that law enforcement practices today are motivated by impermissible discriminatory intent. It is one factor to consider, however, especially given the evidence that, among some in Ferguson, these attitudes persist today. As courts have instructed, the historical background of an official practice that leads to discriminatory effects is, together with other evidence, probative as to whether that practice is grounded in part in discriminatory purposes. *See Vill. of Arlington Heights*, 429 U.S. at 267; *see also Rogers v. Lodge*, 458 U.S. 613, *passim* (1982).

> e.   Failure to Evaluate or Correct Practices that Have Long Resulted in a
>   Racially Disparate Impact

That the discriminatory effect of Ferguson's law enforcement practices is the result of intentional discrimination is further evidenced by the fact that City, police, and court officials have consistently failed to evaluate or reform—and in fact appear to have redoubled their commitment to—the very practices that have plainly and consistently exerted a disparate impact on African Americans.

---

7 Richard Rothstein, *The Making of Ferguson*, Econ. Policy Inst. (Oct. 2014), *available at* http://www.epi.org/publication/making-ferguson/.

The disparities we have identified appear to be longstanding. The statistical analysis performed as part of our investigation relied upon police and court data from recent years, but FPD has collected data related to vehicle stops pursuant to state requirements since 2000. Each year, that information is gathered by FPD, sent to the office of the Missouri Attorney General, and published on the Missouri Attorney General's webpage.[8] The data show disparate impact on African Americans in Ferguson for as long as that data has been reported. Based on that racial profiling data, Missouri publishes a "Disparity Index" for each reporting municipality, calculated as the percent of stops of a certain racial group compared with that group's local population rate. In each of the last 14 years, the data show that African Americans are "over represented" in FPD's vehicular stops.[9] That data also shows that in most years, FPD officers searched African Americans at higher rates than others, but found contraband on African Americans at lower rates.

In 2001, for example, African Americans comprised about the same proportion of the population as whites, but while stops of white drivers accounted for 1,495 stops, African Americans accounted for 3,426, more than twice as many. While a white person stopped that year was searched in 6% of cases, a black person stopped was searched in 14% of cases. That same year, searches of whites resulted in a contraband finding in 21% of cases, but searches of African Americans only resulted in a contraband finding in 16% of cases. Similar disparities were identified in most other years, with varying degrees of magnitude. In any event, the data reveals a pattern of racial disparities in Ferguson's police activities. That pattern appears to have been ignored by Ferguson officials.

That the extant racial disparities are intentional is also evident in the fact that Ferguson has consistently returned to the unlawful practices described in Parts III.A. and B. of this Report knowing that they impose a persistent disparate impact on African Americans. . . .

* * * * *

Based on this evidence, it is apparent that FPD requires better training, limits on officer discretion, increased supervision, and more robust accountability systems, not only to ensure that officers act in accordance with the Fourth Amendment, but with the Fourteenth Amendment as well. FPD has failed to take any such corrective action, and instead has actively endorsed and encouraged the perpetuation of the practices that have led to such stark disparities. This, together with the totality of the facts that we have found, evidences that those practices exist, at least in part, on account of an unconstitutional discriminatory purpose. *See* [*Personnel Adm'r of Mass. v.*] *Feeney*, 442 U.S. [256] at 279 n.24 [(1979)] (noting that the discriminatory intent inquiry is "practical," because what "any official entity is 'up to' may be plain from the results its actions achieve, or the results they avoid").

---

8 *See Missouri Vehicle Stops Report*, Missouri Attorney General, http://ago.mo.gov/VehicleStops/ Reports.php?lea=161 (last visited Feb. 13, 2015).

9 Data for the entire state of Missouri shows an even higher "Disparity Index" for those years than the disparity index present in Ferguson. This raises, by the state's own metric, considerable concerns about policing outside of Ferguson as well.

D. Ferguson Law Enforcement Practices Erode Community Trust, Especially Among Ferguson's African-American Residents, and Make Policing Less Effective, More Difficult, and Less Safe

The unlawful police misconduct and court practices described above have generated great distrust of Ferguson law enforcement, especially among African Americans.[10] As described below, other FPD practices further contribute to distrust, including FPD's failure to hold officers accountable for misconduct, failure to implement community policing principles, and the lack of diversity within FPD. Together, these practices severely damaged the relationship between African Americans and the Ferguson Police Department long before Michael Brown's shooting death in August 2014. This divide has made policing in Ferguson less effective, more difficult, and more likely to discriminate.

* * * * *

A growing body of research, alongside decades of police experience, is consistent with what our investigation found in Ferguson: that when police and courts treat people unfairly, unlawfully, or disrespectfully, law enforcement loses legitimacy in the eyes of those who have experienced, or even observed, the unjust conduct. *See, e.g.*, Tom R. Tyler & Yuen J. Huo, *Trust in the Law: Encouraging Public Cooperation with the Police and Courts* (2002). Further, this loss of legitimacy makes individuals more likely to resist enforcement efforts and less likely to cooperate with law enforcement efforts to prevent and investigate crime. *See, e.g.*, Jason Sunshine & Tom R. Tyler, *The Role of Procedural Justice and Legitimacy in Shaping Public Support for Policing*, 37 Law & Soc'y Rev. 513, 534-36 (2003); *Promoting Cooperative Strategies to Reduce Racial Profiling* 20-21 (U.S. Dep't of Justice, Office of Community Oriented Policing Services, 2008) ("Being viewed as fair and just is critical to successful policing in a democracy. When the police are perceived as unfair in their enforcement, it will undermine their effectiveness."); Ron Davis et al., *Exploring the Role of the Police in Prisoner Reentry* 13-14 (Nat'l Inst. of Justice, New Perspectives in Policing, July 2012) ("Increasingly, research is supporting the notion that legitimacy is an important factor in the effectiveness of law, and the establishment and maintenance of legitimacy are particularly important in the context of policing.") (citations omitted). To improve community trust and police effectiveness, Ferguson must ensure not only that its officers act in accord with the Constitution, but that they treat people fairly and respectfully.

* * * * *

---

10 Although beyond the scope of this investigation, it appears clear that individuals' experiences with other law enforcement agencies in St. Louis County, including with the police departments in surrounding municipalities and the County Police, in many instances have contributed to a general distrust of law enforcement that impacts interactions with the Ferguson police and municipal court.

4.   FPD's Failure to Respond to Complaints of Officer Misconduct Further Erodes Community Trust

Public trust has been further eroded by FPD's lack of any meaningful system for holding officers accountable when they violate law or policy. Through its system for taking, investigating, and responding to misconduct complaints, a police department has the opportunity to demonstrate that officer misconduct is unacceptable and unrepresentative of how the law enforcement agency values and treats its constituents. In this way, a police department's internal affairs process provides an opportunity for the department to restore trust and affirm its legitimacy. Similarly, misconduct investigations allow law enforcement the opportunity to provide community members who have been mistreated a constructive, effective way to voice their complaints. And, of course, effective internal affairs processes can be a critical part of correcting officer behavior, and improving police training and policies.

Ferguson's internal affairs system fails to respond meaningfully to complaints of officer misconduct. It does not serve as a mechanism to restore community members' trust in law enforcement, or correct officer behavior. Instead, it serves to contrast FPD's tolerance for officer misconduct against the Department's aggressive enforcement of even minor municipal infractions, lending credence to a sentiment that we heard often from Ferguson residents: that a "different set of rules" applies to Ferguson's police than to its African-American residents, and that making a complaint about officer misconduct is futile.

Despite the statement in FPD's employee misconduct investigation policy that "[t]he integrity of the police department depends on the personal integrity and discipline of each employee," FPD has done little to investigate external allegations that officers have not followed FPD policy or the law, or, with a few notable exceptions, to hold officers accountable when they have not. Ferguson Police Department makes it difficult to make complaints about officer conduct, and frequently assumes that the officer is telling the truth and the complainant is not, even where objective evidence indicates that the reverse is true.

It is difficult for individuals to make a misconduct complaint against an officer in Ferguson, in part because Ferguson both discourages individuals from making complaints and discourages City and police staff from accepting them.

* * * * *

Even when individuals do report misconduct, there is a significant likelihood it will not be treated as a complaint and investigated.

* * * * *

FPD appears to intentionally *not* treat allegations of misconduct as complaints even where it believes that the officer in fact committed the misconduct.

* * * * *

Even where a complaint is actually investigated, unless the complaint is made by an FPD commander, and sometimes not even then, FPD consistently takes the word of the officer over the word of the complainant, frequently even where the officer's version of events is clearly at odds with the objective evidence. On the rare occasion that FPD does sustain an external complaint of officer misconduct, the discipline it imposes is generally too low to be an effective deterrent.

Our investigation raised concerns in particular about how FPD responds to untruthfulness by officers. In many departments, a finding of untruthfulness pursuant to internal investigation results in an officer's termination because the officer's credibility on police reports and in providing testimony is subsequently subject to challenge. In FPD, untruthfulness appears not even to always result in a formal investigation, and even where sustained, has little effect.

* * * * *

By failing to hold officers accountable, FPD leadership sends a message that FPD officers can behave as they like, regardless of law or policy, and even if caught, that punishment will be light. This message serves to condone officer misconduct and fuel community distrust.

5.   FPD's Lack of Community Engagement Increases the Likelihood of Discriminatory Policing and Damages Public Trust

Alongside its divisive law enforcement practices and lack of meaningful response to community concerns about police conduct, FPD has made little effort in recent years to employ community policing or other community engagement strategies. This lack of community engagement has precluded the possibility of bridging the divide caused by Ferguson's law enforcement practices, and has increased the likelihood of discriminatory policing.

Community policing and related community engagement strategies provide the opportunity for officers and communities to work together to identify the causes of crime and disorder particular to their community, and to prioritize law enforcement efforts. *See Community Policing Defined* 1-16 (U.S. Dep't of Justice, Office of Community Oriented Policing Services, 2014). The focus of these strategies—in stark contrast to Ferguson's current law enforcement approach—is on crime prevention rather than on making arrests. *See Effective Policing and Crime Prevention: A Problem Oriented Guide for Mayors, City Managers, and County Executives* 1-62 (U.S. Dep't of Justice, Office of Community Oriented Policing Services, 2009). When implemented fully, community policing creates opportunities for officers and community members to have frequent, positive interactions with each other, and requires officers to partner with communities to solve particular public safety problems that, together, they have decided to address. Research and experience show that community policing can be more effective at crime prevention and at making people feel safer. *See* Gary Cordner, *Reducing Fear of Crime: Strategies for Police* 47 (U.S. Dep't of Justice, Office of Community Oriented Policing Services, Jan. 2010) ("Most studies of community policing have found that residents like community policing and feel safer when it is implemented where they live and work.") (citations omitted).

* * * * *

Ferguson's community policing efforts appear always to have been somewhat modest, but have dwindled to almost nothing in recent years. FPD has no community policing or community engagement plan. FPD currently designates a single officer the "Community Resource Officer." This officer attends community meetings, serves as FPD's public relations liaison, and is charged with collecting crime data. No other officers play any substantive role in community policing efforts.

* * * * *

V. CHANGES NECESSARY TO REMEDY FERGUSON'S UNLAWFUL LAW ENFORCEMENT PRACTICES AND REPAIR COMMUNITY TRUST

The problems identified within this letter reflect deeply entrenched practices and priorities that are incompatible with lawful and effective policing and that damage community trust. Addressing those problems and repairing the City's relationship with the community will require a fundamental redirection of Ferguson's approach to law enforcement, including the police and court practices that reflect and perpetuate this approach.

Below we set out broad recommendations for changes that Ferguson should make to its police and court practices to correct the constitutional violations our investigation identified. Ensuring meaningful, sustainable, and verifiable reform will require that these and other measures be part of a court-enforceable remedial process that includes involvement from community stakeholders as well as independent oversight. In the coming weeks, we will seek to work with the City of Ferguson toward developing and reaching agreement on an appropriate framework for reform.

A.   Ferguson Police Practices

1.   Implement a Robust System of True Community Policing

Many of the recommendations included below would require a shift from policing to raise revenue to policing in partnership with the entire Ferguson community. Developing these relationships will take time and considerable effort. FPD should:

> a.   Develop and put into action a policy and detailed plan for comprehensive implementation of community policing and problem-solving principles. Conduct outreach and involve the entire community in developing and implementing this plan;

* * * * *

2. Focus Stop, Search, Ticketing and Arrest Practices on Community Protection

FPD must fundamentally change the way it conducts stops and searches, issues citations and summonses, and makes arrests. FPD officers must be trained and required to abide by the law. In addition, FPD enforcement efforts should be reoriented so that officers are required to take enforcement action because it promotes public safety, not simply because they have legal authority to act. To do this, FPD should:

  a.   Prohibit the use of ticketing and arrest quotas, whether formal or informal;

  b.   Require that officers report in writing all stops, searches and arrests, including pedestrian stops, and that their reports articulate the legal authority for the law enforcement action and sufficient description of facts to support that authority;

* * * * *

3. Increase Tracking, Review, and Analysis of FPD Stop, Search, Ticketing and Arrest Practices

At the first level of supervision and as an agency, FPD must review more stringently officers' stop, search, ticketing, and arrest practices to ensure that officers are complying with the Constitution and department policy, and to evaluate the impact of officer activity on police legitimacy and community trust. FPD should:

  a.   Develop and implement a plan for broader collection of stop, search, ticketing, and arrest data that includes pedestrian stops, enhances vehicle stop data collection, and requires collection of data on all stop and post-stop activity, as well as location and demographic information;

  b.   Require supervisors to review all officer activity and review all officer reports before the supervisor leaves shift;

  c.   Develop and implement system for regular review of stop, search, ticketing, and arrest data at supervisory and agency level to detect problematic trends and ensure consistency with public safety and community policing goals;

  d.   Analyze race and other disparities shown in stop, search, ticketing, and arrest practices to determine whether disparities can be reduced consistent with public safety goals.

4. Change Force Use, Reporting, Review, and Response to Encourage De-Escalation and the Use of the Minimal Force Necessary in a Situation

FPD should reorient officers' approach to using force by ensuring that they are trained and skilled in using tools and tactics to de-escalate situations, and incentivized to avoid using force wherever possible. FPD also should implement a system of force review that ensures that improper force is detected and responded to effectively, and that policy, training, tactics, and officer safety concerns are identified.

* * * * *

7. <u>Implement Measures to Reduce Bias and Its Impact on Police Behavior</u>

Many of the recommendations listed elsewhere have the potential to reduce the level and impact of bias on police behavior (e.g., increasing positive interactions between police and the community; increasing the collection and analysis of stop data; and increasing oversight of the exercise of police discretion). Below are additional measures that can assist in this effort. FPD should:

a. Provide initial and recurring training to all officers that sends a clear, consistent and emphatic message that bias-based profiling and other forms of discriminatory policing are prohibited. Training should include:

1) Relevant legal and ethical standards;

2) Information on how stereotypes and implicit bias can infect police work;

3) The importance of procedural justice and police legitimacy on community trust, police effectiveness, and officer safety;

4) The negative impacts of profiling on public safety and crime prevention;

b. Provide training to supervisors and commanders on detecting and responding to bias- based profiling and other forms of discriminatory policing;

c. Include community members from groups that have expressed high levels of distrust of police in officer training;

d. Take steps to eliminate all forms of workplace bias from FPD and the City.

* * * * *

10. <u>Improve Officer Supervision</u>

The recommendations set out here cannot be implemented without dedicated, skilled, and well- trained supervisors who police lawfully and without bias. FPD should:

a. Provide all supervisors with specific supervisory training prior to assigning them to supervisory positions;

b. Develop and require supervisors to use an "early intervention system" to objectively detect problematic patterns of officer misconduct, assist officers who need additional attention, and identify training and equipment needs;

c.   Support supervisors who encourage and guide respectful policing and implement community policing principles, and evaluate them on this basis. Remove supervisors who do not adequately review officer activity and reports or fail to support, through words or actions, unbiased policing;

d.   Ensure that an adequate number of qualified first-line supervisors are deployed in the field to allow supervisors to provide close and effective supervision to each officer under the supervisor's direct command, provide officers with the direction and guidance necessary to improve and develop as officers, and to identify, correct, and prevent misconduct.

* * * * *

12.   **Develop Mechanisms to More Effectively Respond to Allegations of Officer Misconduct**

Responding to allegations of officer misconduct is critical not only to correct officer behavior and identify policy, training, or tactical concerns, but also to build community confidence and police legitimacy. FPD should:

a.   Modify procedures and practices for accepting complaints to make it easier and less intimidating for individuals to register formal complaints about police conduct, including providing complaint forms online and in various locations throughout the City and allowing for complaints to be submitted online and by third parties or anonymously;

b.   Require that all complaints be logged and investigated;

c.   Develop and implement a consistent, reliable, and fair process for investigating and responding to complaints of officer misconduct. As part of this process, FPD should:

    1)   Investigate all misconduct complaints, even where the complainant indicates he or she does not want the complaint investigated, or wishes to remain anonymous;

    2)   Not withdraw complaints without reaching a disposition;

d.   Develop and implement a fair and consistent system for disciplining officers found to have committed misconduct;

e.   Terminate officers found to have been materially untruthful in performance of their duties, including in completing reports or during internal affairs investigations;

f.   Timely provide in writing to the Ferguson Prosecuting Attorney all impeachment information on officers who may testify or provide sworn reports, including findings of untruthfulness in internal affairs investigations, for disclosure to the defendant under *Brady v. Maryland*, 373 U.S. 83 (1963);

g.   Document in a central location all misconduct complaints and investigations, including the nature of the complaint, the name of the officer, and the disposition of the investigation;

h.   Maintain complete misconduct complaint investigative files in a central location;

i.   Develop and implement a community-centered mediation program to resolve, as appropriate, allegations of officer misconduct.

* * * * *

V.   CONCLUSION

Our investigation indicates that Ferguson as a City has the capacity to reform its approach to law enforcement. A small municipal department may offer greater potential for officers to form partnerships and have frequent, positive interactions with Ferguson residents, repairing and maintaining police-community relationships. *See, e.g.*, Jim Burack, *Putting the "Local" Back in Local Law Enforcement, in, American Policing in 2022: Essays on the Future of the Profession* 79-83 (Debra R. Cohen McCullough & Deborah L. Spence, eds., 2012). These reform efforts will be well worth the considerable time and dedication they will require, as they have the potential to make Ferguson safer and more united.

THOMAS A. GOFORTH
Curriculum Vitae

CURRENT EMPLOYMENT

YR-1 to present   United States Air Force Central Action Officer
for Non-Lethal Weapons
USAF HQ Security Forces Center
San Antonio, TX

YR-2 to present   Consultant, American Civil Liberties Union
National Office
Community Policing/Racial Profiling Project

YR-2 to present   Motivational Speaker, Keppler Associates

EDUCATION

PhD Urban Studies/Criminology, Nita State University (YR-10)
Master of Public Administration, Nita State University (YR-12)
Bachelor of Arts, United States History, University of Alabama (YR-28)

LAW ENFORCEMENT EMPLOYMENT

YR-14 to YR-2	Chief of Police, Downingtown, Nita
YR-20 to YR-14	Chief of Police, City of Montgomery, AL
YR-21 to YR-20	Deputy Chief of Operations, City of Montgomery, AL
YR-22 to YR-21	Captain of the North Precinct, Montgomery, AL
YR-28 to YR-22	Patrol Officer-Sergeant-Lieutenant, Montgomery AL

HIGHER EDUCATION EMPLOYMENT

YR-4 to YR-2	Adjunct Faculty—Criminal Justice—Nita Community College
YR-9 to YR-5	Adjunct Faculty—Criminal Justice—Nita State University

UNITED STATES MILITARY

YR-14 to present   Nita Air National Guard–Major
Commander of 14th Security Forces Squadron

YR-21 to YR-14   Alabama Air National Guard–Logistics, Plans Officer

SELECTED PRESENTATIONS-KEYNOTES-PANELS

March 5, YR-1   Keynote: The Role of Police and the Hispanic Community
Hispanic Chamber of Commerce Awards Dinner
Harrisburg, Nita

April 23, YR-1	American Style Policing and the Refugee/Immigrant Community
	3rd Annual Conference on Refugees
	Nita State University
February 27, YR-1	Panel: Data Collection, with Philip Carson, Superintendent of the New Jersey State Police
	Region One Annual Training Conference
	Atlantic City, New Jersey
September 10, YR-2	Data Collection: Role in Racial Profiling
	New York Attorney General's Public Dialogue
	New York, New York
July 30, YR-2	Panel: Challenges and Opportunities in Being a Chief Law Enforcement Executive
	National Organization of Chiefs of Police
	25th Annual Training Conference
October 8, YR-4	Panel: Color/Racial Profiling
	National Conference on the Impact of Race and Ethnicity on the Justice System
	American Bar Association Council on Racial and Ethnic Justice
	Los Angeles, CA
August 21, YR-6	Community Policing and Its Relationship to Building Stronger, Healthier Communities
	HUD Community First Leadership Program
	Ohio State University
	Columbus, Ohio

PUBLICATIONS

Evaluating Community Policing, THE POLICE CHIEF, Vol. LXVII, No. 3, March YR-3

Preventing Profiling through Data Collection, co-authored with Wendy Lin and Steve Stipak, PhD, JOURNAL OF THE INTERNATIONAL ASSOCIATION OF CHIEFS OF POLICE, November YR-4

AWARDS

NE Coalition for the Prevention of Crime, Neighborhood Community Policing Award (YR-11)

West Coast Black Publishers Award for Outstanding Service in Law Enforcement (YR-9)

Nita Association of Chiefs of Police Service Award (YR-8)

Alabama Association of Chiefs of Police President's Award (YR-17)

Nita University
School of Law

Professor Neil L. Ellman
9536 W. Arapahoe
Nita City, Nita 09102

David Payton, Esq.
Payton and Payton
P.O. Box 1976
3513 North Front Street
Nita City, Nita 09102

January 15, YR-0

Re: Stucky v. Conlee et al.

Dear Mr. Payton:

At your request, I have reviewed the following documents for review in the above captioned case:

1) Complaint;

2) Answer;

3) Clayton Stucky's deposition transcript;

4) Officer Conlee's and Officer Parsell's deposition transcripts;

5) Chief of Police Lieber's deposition transcript;

6) Officer Conlee's past employment reviews as to the category of "lack of prejudice" with the Nita Township Police Department;

7) The City of Nita Police Department's Rules, Policies, and Procedures Manual;

8) City of Nita Police Department Traffic Enforcement Training Manual;

9) City of Nita Police Department Training Division Traffic Study; and

10) Expert Report of Dr. Charles Goforth.

As we agreed, I am charging $300 per hour to review the documents and write reports, and $450 per hour for time that I spend testifying or waiting to testify.

A. Opinion and Reasoning

After a thorough review of all the documents, it is my conclusion that Dr. Goforth is incorrect. There is insufficient evidence to conclude that either the officers involved in the stop of Mr. Stucky or

Nita City should be liable in this case. This opinion follows from not just a review of the documents presented, but also a review of the applicable law.

I first note that Dr. Goforth never concluded that Officers Conlee and Parsell stopped Mr. Stucky because of his race. I do not believe that any expert could review this file and reliably conclude that the officers used Mr. Stucky's race as a basis for the stop, although I do not view these facts as representative of a typical case of profiling because the stop was done in the course of training rather than as a law enforcement activity. Dr. Goforth also accepts Trooper Stucky's recounting of the stop over the contrary version related by Officers Conlee and Parsell. And the traffic study, while not ideal in its methodology, does not support a pattern of profiling in traffic enforcement by Conlee, Parsell, or the Nita City Police Department.

In my view, Dr. Goforth feels that the facts, as they emerge from the documents and the testimony, show an insufficient responsiveness on the part of Chief of Police Lieber to the issue of racial profiling, as Dr. Goforth understands that concept. By overlying the policies he finds inadequate with a large number of general statements about the problem—as well as his personal beliefs—he concludes that Chief Lieber was deliberately indifferent. He also implicitly, and uncritically, assumes the truth of the facts as reported by plaintiff Stucky, while disregarding contrary evidence provided by the officers. At least as important, Dr. Goforth proceeds from an incorrect understanding of the legal standard governing the liability of the City: "deliberate indifference." For these reasons, his opinion is incorrect, and the City should not be found liable for violating Mr. Stucky's constitutional rights.

The liability of the City in this case turns on the standard of deliberate indifference. To be liable under Section 1983 for unconstitutional acts resulting from inadequate policies, training, or supervision, the deficiency in policy, training, or supervision must reflect an intentional disregard for the possibility of violation; this indifference must be shown to have caused the violation. Liability may be imposed on a municipality upon a showing of deliberate indifference exhibited by a pattern of inadequate policies, training, supervision, and discipline of police officers, provided that there is a causal connection between such inadequacies and the risk of harm to others.

Reviewing the opinion of Dr. Goforth, what strikes one repeatedly is that he takes small grains of fact from the depositions—e.g., that Officer Conlee is a training officer, that Chief Lieber's department does not keep statistics on traffic stops and searches, that the Code of Ethics does not specifically mention racial profiling—and puts all of this together to construct a narrative. This narrative is woven into a larger narrative of things that Dr. Goforth knows, has read about, or (in one unfortunate instance in Mobile, Alabama) experienced himself, to show that racial profiling is a real phenomenon, that it has been an issue in law enforcement for some years, and that therefore failure to do more proves a violation of law. In no part of this story does Dr. Goforth tell us the professional standards by which he measures law enforcement action on this issue. He does not tell us where it is established, in case law, statute, or the professional literature, that the law enforcement Code of Ethics (reproduced in the Traffic Training Manual) is insufficient for this task. Rather, we are told that Dr. Goforth knows a lot, has been around, has heard and talked about the issue a lot, and therefore the court should take his word for it. As impressive as his background is, this does not come close to establishing a basis for an expert opinion as I understand it from teaching the law of Evidence. *See, e.g.,* Fed. R. Evid. 702(c); *Daubert v. Merrill Dow,* 509 U.S. 579 (1993).

I agree with Dr. Goforth on some fundamental points stated in his report. First, I strongly agree that racial profiling—police use of racial or ethnic appearance, among other factors, to decide which people to consider suspicious and to stop, frisk, question, or otherwise initiate police action—is real. It exists in American law enforcement (though not in every police department by any means); it has existed for years; and it is a measurable phenomenon in some police departments. Dr. Goforth is entirely correct that racial profiling is harmful both to the victim and to the effectiveness and safety of law enforcement officials. Second, many police departments have taken action on the problem by creating and implementing policies specific to the issue, and by creating training for officers on the issue. Third, some police departments collect data on traffic stops and searches associated with them.

Nevertheless, while it might have been better and reasonable for the City of Nita Police Department to have specific policies, training, and data collection on racial profiling, I believe Dr. Goforth significantly overstates the case when he says the department was deliberately indifferent and violated Mr. Stucky's constitutional rights by not doing these things. While the most current research is a few years old, a study by Fridell and colleagues at the Police Executive Research Forum (PERF), a leading voice for research-based excellence and best practices in policing, found that it is not the case that all departments—even among the largest ones in the United States—had policies or training specific to racial profiling. Many professional organizations, including PERF and the International Association of Chiefs of Police, have had available since at least YR-15 model policies that a police agency can utilize as a starting point for constructing such policies. But none of these organizations specify that their member organizations or officers must have such a policy or must have racial profiling training.

Dr. Goforth relies heavily on the United States Department of Justice Investigation of the Ferguson Police Department (DOJ Ferguson Report). The DOJ Ferguson Report not only fails to support a conclusion that Chief Lieber was deliberately indifferent; it confirms that there is insufficient evidence here to prove that Chief Lieber was deliberately indifferent to the risk that his officers would engage in bias-based policing.

First, the magnitude of the DOJ investigation into Ferguson is indicative of the type of data that would be needed to support a finding of deliberate indifference in NITA City. DOJ interviewed the City Manager, Mayor, Chief of Police, Municipal Judge, Municipal Court Clerk, City Finance Manager, and half of the Police Department's sworn officers. DOJ spent 108 person-days onsite, participated in ride-alongs, reviewed tens of thousands of pages of police records, and used statistical experts to analyze Ferguson Police Department data. DOJ also extended its investigation into the local community.

One would not insist or expect that an individual citizen alleging racial profiling would have the resources to conduct an investigation as comprehensive as Ferguson. And unlike the State of Nita, Missouri law required the Ferguson Police Department to collect race and other data for every traffic stop. Nonetheless, the absence of *any* evidence of a pattern of disparate use of race in traffic stops by the Nita City Police—and the refutation of any such pattern by the only available empirical evidence (the Traffic Study)—undermines Dr. Goforth's opinion that Chief Lieber was deliberately indifferent.

Furthermore, the DOJ Report found that bias-based policing in Ferguson was caused by a desire to generate revenue, a fact reinforced by the actions of the municipal court. Nowhere does Dr. Goforth suggest that financial pressure played a role in the action of any government actor in Nita City.

The DOJ Report finding that Ferguson officials engaged in intentional discrimination was based on the entirety of evidence, most of which is absent in Nita City. Statistical analyses demonstrated race-based disparities in *every* aspect of Ferguson police operations. Law enforcement personnel expressed discriminatory views in email messages and during interviews. Ferguson officials displayed racial stereotyping by their view that "lack of personal responsibility" among African-Americans was the root cause of their disproportionate interactions with law enforcement. Ferguson was historically a racially segregated community, with some residents clinging to attitudes that supported segregation. It is against this full complex of factors that the DOJ found the failure of Ferguson to evaluate or correct practices evidenced discriminatory intent. By contrast, there is *no* evidence of *any* of these factors in Nita City.

The United States government, in various white papers and other documents issued through agencies of the DOJ, has not required that police agencies that receive federal funds adopt policies or training programs, and has not required the collection of data. In fact, legislation has been introduced in every session of Congress for twelve years (all titled "The End Racial Profiling Act") that would have required policy, training, and data collection as a condition of federal funding; the bills have failed to be enacted into law each time. (The State of Nita has never considered, much less adopted, such a requirement.)

In short, while some police departments do have specific policies, training modules, and the like on racial profiling, and some smaller number collect data, most do not. There are roughly 17,000 law enforcement agencies in the United States; to put it simply, if the Nita City Police Department is deliberately indifferent to the constitutional rights of the plaintiff, so are most police departments throughout the country. The DOJ Ferguson Report confirms that Chief Lieber's failure to adopt policies and training would not be considered cause, in the legal sense, if his officers engaged in profiling. Resolving the problem of bias-based policing in Ferguson required more than policies and training on profiling. The DOJ recommendations required a shift from policing as a means to raise revenue to policing as a partnership with the entire Ferguson community, including a detailed plan for comprehensive implementation of community policing and problem-solving principles. The DOJ Ferguson Report further issued several recommendations designed to prevent excessive force, which is neither a documented problem in Nita City nor part of Mr. Stucky's claim in this case. Again, it is only when a chief of police is on notice that his officers are engaged in a pattern of constitutional violation that his failure to respond by policy or training can be deemed to be a cause of subsequent violations of the Constitution.

B. Summary

Overall, I find Dr. Goforth's opinion uninformed by the research and insufficiently grounded in the law that guides policing efforts. I do not denigrate his opinions or devalue his lived experiences. On the contrary, I share some of his beliefs. But in this case, the evidence does not support his opinion about the liability of Nita City.

Very truly yours,

/s/ Neil Ellman
Professor of Law

Professor Neil L. Ellman

Employment:

YR-5 to present

Professor of Law
    Nita School of Law
    Courses taught include Evidence, Section 1983 Litigation,
    Criminal Procedure, Criminal Law

YR-5 to YR-7

Assistant Federal Defender
    Federal Defender for the Eastern District of Nita

YR-10 to YR-7

Assistant Public Defender
    Office of Public Defender
    Nita County

YR-11 to YR-10

Law Clerk
    Hon. Emilia Ortiz
    United States District Court
    Eastern District of Nita

Education:

JD, Stanford Law School YR-11
Honors: Order of the Coif

BA, University of Wisconsin YR-14
Honors: Phi Beta Kappa

Selected Publications:

Driving While Black: Perceptions and Reality, 53 Northwestern L. Rev. 570 (YR-1)

Pretext, Profiling and Prevention, 79 Michigan Journal of Law Reform 28 (YR-2)

Subjectivity and Objectivity: The Supreme Court's Evolving Fourth Amendment Paradigm, 34 Emory L. J. 644 (YR-3)

Empiricism and Law Enforcement, 18 Kansas L. Rev. 499 (YR-4)

Academic and Professional Conferences:

Panelist, Deconstructing the Prism of Profiling, AALS Section on Civil Rights (YR-2)

Invited Presenter, Symposium on Driving While Black, Boalt Law School (YR-3)

Legislative Testimony:

I have testified four times before the United States Congress and various state legislatures on the issue of racial profiling.

Court Testimony:

I have served as an expert witness in four civil cases that centered on the issue of racial profiling, twice as the expert for the plaintiff and twice as the expert for the defense.

MEDICAL EXPERT REPORTS

December 1, YR-1

**Collins & Associates
8 Wyntre Brooke Drive
Elmerton, Nita 09103**

Attorney Sharon K. Coby
ACLU
105 North Front Street, Suite 225
Nita City, Nita 09101

Re: Clayton Stucky

Dear Ms. Coby:

This letter sets forth my treatment of Clayton Stucky, my diagnosis of his medical condition, and my opinion as to the cause of that condition. Because Mr. Stucky is a patient, I am not charging for this letter. My fee to testify in court is $250 per hour.

I have been a licensed clinical psychologist for nineteen years. I specialize in health psychology: treating and addressing a variety of conditions involving the mind/body relationship. The bulk of my practice involves treating patients. For the past thirteen years, I have also spent eleven hours a week serving as a consultant to the Bureau of Disability Determination for the Social Security Administration. In that capacity, I review applicants' medical records in order to make psychological determinations. A true and accurate copy of my curriculum vitae is attached to this report.

Clayton Stucky was referred to me for evaluation and counseling in March of YR-1 by Dr. Anna Stovall, who is Mr. Stucky's family doctor. Mr. Stucky sought treatment with Dr. Stovall on December 1 of YR-2 because of persistent migraines. Dr. Stovall's records indicated that Mr. Stucky has suffered from migraine headaches since YR-3. The headaches started while he was under a grand jury investigation, which frightened him and made him paranoid. Since that time, Mr. Stucky has been on medication for migraines. However, the migraine headaches became more frequent and more severe following the August YR-2 traffic stop. Previous to that incident, Mr. Stucky experienced migraines once every few weeks. In the week preceding our first appointment, he had experienced three migraines. Mr. Stucky also lost weight, as he could not eat because his stomach was "knotted up." He had difficulty sleeping because of the headaches and accompanying

**(332) 555-3827
collinsmedical.nita**

nausea. Dr. Stovall assessed Mr. Stucky as having worsening migraines and prescribed Imitrex for the migraine headaches.

Dr. Stovall's progress note of December 22, YR-2 indicated that Mr. Stucky's girlfriend called her very concerned about Mr. Stucky's safety, describing a decreased appetite, a decreased libido, and a changed personality.

Dr. Stovall's note of December 26, YR-2 indicated Mr. Stucky reported a depressed mood, shorter temper, anhedonia (the loss of pleasure), and that he was unable to concentrate on his job. Dr. Stovall noted that Mr. Stucky sat slouched in the exam room with diminished eye contact and decreased affect and mood. Dr. Stovall assessed Mr. Stucky as having situational anxiety and depression. She prescribed Lexapro, which is an antidepressant. Dr. Stovall suggested that Mr. Stucky consult me because she believed Mr. Stucky's conditions were related to situational stressors that a psychologist could better address.

I saw Mr. Stucky initially on March 22, YR-1. In the course of treatment, we met on April 1, April 9, April 15, April 19, April 28, June 10, July 7, July 15, July 30, October 18, November 1, and November 11, YR-1.

The initial interview lasted approximately an hour and fifteen minutes. Mr. Stucky provided his medical records from Dr. Stovall, outlining the information she had gathered.

Mr. Stucky seemed reluctant to come in for treatment. Most men are not inclined to view counseling as an acceptable intervention to solve their problems, and are uncomfortable accepting outside assistance. Mr. Stucky had not sought or received psychological help before August of YR-2. He reported difficulty sleeping and loss of appetite. Mr. Stucky related the details of being stopped for a traffic violation by Officers Conlee and Parsell. Mr. Stucky felt that he was stopped solely because he is an African-American. He said the officers demanded his license and registration aggressively and yelled at him. Mr. Stucky did not report any physical altercation. He recalled comforting his girlfriend and using his cell phone to contact his sergeant for assistance. Mr. Stucky acknowledged feeling bewildered and perplexed by the officers' behavior. It wasn't until Mr. Stucky allowed his gold shield to be visibly exposed that the officers backed off. Mr. Stucky subsequently felt angry and betrayed. Unrelated to the traffic incident, Mr. Stucky also mentioned that he had been divorced for four or five years.

I made three diagnoses after the initial visit: 1) posttraumatic stress disorder (PTSD) in a chronic phase; 2) an adjustment disorder with mixed emotional features; and 3) psychological factors affecting physical condition. I arrived at the diagnosis of PTSD because, based on the incident that transpired in his traffic stop, Mr. Stucky had felt threatened, had felt unsafe, and could not comprehend why anyone, especially a fellow law enforcement official would behave or interact in such a manner. Mr. Stucky felt fearful as he attempted to provide appropriate identification to the officers. He specifically referenced instances of African-Americans stopped in traffic who, while securing their identifying information, were actually shot. He felt threatened by the situation. He felt concerned for his girlfriend's welfare, who was emotionally distressed, and that concern fostered Stucky's own attempts to make sense of the situation. When he could not, he clearly presented with the sense of helplessness and the sense that he had been reduced—to use his own words— "to feeling like a nobody at that point."

I had never previously treated a patient for PTSD arising out of a traffic stop. PTSD usually arises from events that would be outside the range of common experience. While some physical trauma may occur, it is not a required criterion for a diagnosis of PTSD. Speaking in a loud manner or yelling may be a necessary component of creating PTSD, but would not suffice alone to come to that diagnosis. Mr. Stucky never indicated that either officer struck him physically or pulled out his gun, though he did note that Officer Parsell had his hand at the ready. Even though no threat was verbalized to him, Mr. Stucky felt threatened because he was not able to comprehend why he was being stopped. He could not understand why the officers would not give him a legitimate reason for the stop; from his unique position as an African-American law enforcement officer, he was fearful of the officers' reaction to his attempt to retrieve identification from his glove compartment, knowing that other African-Americans had been shot while doing nothing more than securing identification.

I am well aware that the general public associates PTSD with returning veterans who have experienced unfathomable trauma in wartime, or victims of sexual abuse. It is particularly difficult for individuals who are not persons of color to comprehend the trauma that follows from instances of discrimination, even when not accompanied by overt threats of physical harm. The most recent edition of the *Diagnostic and Statistical Manual of Mental Disorders (DSM-5)* recognizes that the onset and severity of PTSD differs across cultural groups, though it fails to fully capture the impact, singly and collectively, of micro-aggressions that are the daily plight of persons of color in the United States. This is reflected in the uneasy relationship between citizens of color and the police. While on the one hand reliant on and appreciative of the protection offered by law enforcement, for persons of color every encounter with a police officer poses a potential threat, which is why many persons of color go out of their way to avoid contact with police. One may think that Mr. Stucky, as a police officer primarily tasked with enforcing the motor vehicle code, would be less likely to be traumatized by a traffic stop. In fact, his recognition of the dangers inherent in the most routine stop, where the officer may misinterpret the driver's reaching for identification as an effort to reach for a weapon, and knowing that he had his service weapon in his car, increased Mr. Stucky's concern for his safety. Mr. Stucky's despair over being a victim of discrimination was exacerbated by his recognition that his service to his country and the public did not exempt him from being treated as less than a whole person solely because of his race.

Mr. Stucky had additional symptoms that are required as part of the diagnosis of PTSD. One is recurrent, involuntary, and intrusive re-experiencing of the traumatic event. Mr. Stucky presented with symptoms of intrusive memory. These are moments when a person is not intentionally thinking about the event, but has thoughts thrust upon them in unrelated situations when they are otherwise preoccupied. Mr. Stucky exhibited bad dreams and reported nightmares. He initially had flashbacks, which are traumatic symptoms where the person suddenly, spontaneously, and without warning feels or behaves as if the situation is happening all over again in that moment. He was anxious, restless. He also exhibited avoidance characteristics—attempting to avoid thinking about the incident. Mr. Stucky had given up pleasurable activities, such as his exercise routine. He felt detached from everyone else, including a sense of detachment from all of law enforcement for some period of time.

Mr. Stucky also evidenced the alterations in mood that are a diagnostic criterion of PTSD. Both Mr. Stucky's fiancée and Dr. Stovall noted Mr. Stucky's diminished interest in eating, diminished eye contact, and a depressed affect, as well as decreased interest in pleasurable activities with his fiancée. Mr. Stucky was despondent, worrying whether his son was destined to face discrimination, regardless of his objective achievements, solely because of his race. As noted earlier, Mr. Stucky also manifested difficulty sleeping and found it hard to concentrate on the job. There was no evidence that any of Mr. Stucky's symptoms were due to drug or alcohol use or another medical condition.

State troopers I have worked with over the years, like many law enforcement professionals, learn to keep their emotions under wraps and to think, analyze, and reason. Mr. Stucky could not reason this incident in a way that allowed him to feel better, and so he reluctantly agreed to engage in treatment because he could not tolerate the way he had been feeling any longer.

I diagnosed Mr. Stucky with adjustment disorder because he was having difficulty coping with unforeseen consequences of this lawsuit. Mr. Stucky is a private and reserved individual who does not naturally pursue the limelight. Once this lawsuit was filed, community agencies and media sources bombarded him with requests to give speeches, interviews, and television appearances. These were not something he naturally gravitated to. In addition, Mr. Stucky struggled to cope with the things Officer Conlee was saying in the course of the case. Whether it was naïve or not, Mr. Stucky could not comprehend that a fellow law enforcement officer could act in such a way; he became consumed, spending hours at a time reviewing and poring over deposition testimony because he could not make sense of why this was happening and unfolding the way it was. He was burdened and mentally consumed by the litigation to the point it was affecting him mentally and emotionally. These circumstances would not automatically cause or worsen the specific symptoms of PTSD. But to the extent Mr. Stucky saw, in his own mind, tangible concrete evidence of blatant lies, it undermined his sense of security and safety in what he had held to be essentially sacred about law enforcement. When trust is diminished, trauma has a greater opportunity to breed itself. I attempted to assist Mr. Stucky in adjusting to all of those circumstances.

My treatment of Mr. Stucky included having him retell the story of the incident. I helped him explore his feelings of hurt, fear, anxiety, and anger. Part of the recovery from PTSD requires what most individuals might shy away from doing: going through their narrative and facing the feelings it engenders. I also trained him in diaphragmatic breathing coupled with a cue controlled component to induce a relaxed state. Diaphragmatic breathing is essentially the natural breathing we are born to do—stomach breathing. We often unlearn that and engage in shallow breathing, which triggers arousal rather than relaxation. Diaphragmatic breathing allows for maximum expansion of the lungs and therefore a maximum amount of oxygen circulating through the body, which has a calming effect. The cue controlled component teaches the person to make a statement to themselves as they breathe, such as "Calm" or "I am relaxed," so that as one begins to repeat that over and over, he or she becomes conditioned to feel more relaxed. I also discussed systematic desensitization and guided muscle relaxation routines with Mr. Stucky. In a guided progressive muscle relaxation exercise, the person selectively tenses specific muscle groups in the body for five to seven seconds. Hyper-intensifying the tension exhausts the muscle fiber; upon release, that area of the body becomes calmer and more relaxed, which makes the person feel more in control of oneself. I also encouraged Mr. Stucky to set a time limit for any thinking or paperwork related to his lawsuit, creating a boundary around that activity so that it ceased to impinge on the other parts of his life.

In the course of my treatment of Mr. Stucky, I did have occasion to excuse him from work. A common symptom of PTSD is difficulty with concentration, and Mr. Stucky reported difficulty concentrating even at work. I recall at least one, and possibly two, instances where Mr. Stucky made mistakes that were out of character for him, such as errors in his written reports. He had become so mentally distraught and consumed with what was happening that I recommended a temporary, medical leave of absence. The leave allowed him to pull himself together, get a change of venue, and improve his emotional status so it would not interfere in the performance of his important job duties.

It is my professional opinion, to a reasonable degree of psychological certainty, that Mr. Stucky's PTSD was directly related to the traffic stop of August YR-2.

My opinions are based on my review of Dr. Stovall's records of her treatment of Mr. Stucky as well as my firsthand treatment of Mr. Stucky. I have not met with other witnesses, nor have I reviewed any deposition transcripts.

I am no longer treating Mr. Stucky for posttraumatic stress disorder. By November 11, YR-1, the PTSD symptoms had resolved. I have continued to treat Mr. Stucky for other, unrelated conditions since then.

/s/ *Leslie Collins*
Leslie Collins, PhD

LESLIE COLLINS

20 Ridge Road
Etters, Nita 09105

(322) 555-8305 (home)
(322) 555-4071 (work)
(322) 555-6660 (fax)

Education:

PhD, The University of Health Sciences/
The Chicago Medical School (APA Accredited)
Major: Clinic Psychology
      Health Psychology   6/YR-21

MA, Roosevelt University
Major: Clinical Psychology   9/YR-27

BA, Nita State University
Major: Psychology   5/YR-29

Honors:

Predoctoral internship completed with honors
MA degree conferred with honors

Licensure:

State of Nita #PS-005053-L
State of Nebraska #486 (inactive)

Certification:

Diplomat, American Academy of Pain Management
American Board of Medical Psychotherapists
O.V.R. Qualified – Nita
Surveyor of Chronic Pain Management and Work
Hardening Programs for the Commission on Accreditation of
Rehabilitation Facilities (CARF) (YR-18 – YR-15)

Clinical Experience:

7/YR-17 – Present

Collins & Associates
8 Wyntre Brooke Drive
Elmerton, Nita

- evaluation, psychotherapy and biofeedback services
- clinical supervision, consultation to business and industry
- children, adolescents and adults

5/YR-15 – Present

Social Security Administration
Harristown, Nita
Consultant, Bureau of Disability Determination

1/YR-17 – 11/YR-16

Rehab Hospital of Elmerton
Elmerton, Nita

Director of Pain Rehabilitation
-    developed, implemented and directed a rehabilitation program for

patients with chronic benign pain
- provided in-service training to interdisciplinary treatment team
- conducted evaluations and provided treatment services
- marketed program services to potential referral sources
- administered program function

10/YR-21 – 12/YR-20   Rehab Hospital of Claytown
Claytown, Nita

Director, Department of Medical and Rehabilitation Psychology

Clinical Director, Musculo-Skeletal Injury Rehabilitation Program
- administered department function
- supervised clinical activity of therapists
- provided consultation to General Rehabilitation Services
- provided psychological evaluation and behavior management programming to diverse medical patient population
- provided individual, group, and family therapy to patients with chronic pain
- directed clinical function of treatment team
- participated in Clinical Leadership and Hospital Planning Committee

9/YR-23 – 10/YR-21   University of Nebraska Medical Center
Omaha Nebraska
Staff Psychologist
Pain Management Center

Provided in-patient, day-patient, and out-patient treatment to individuals with chronic benign pain disorders
- conducted individual and group psychotherapy
- conducted short-term marital counseling and family support training
- completed psychological evaluations and psychophysiological stress evaluations
- taught relaxation training and biofeedback
- supervised clinical training of psychology interns and medical students to the Departments of Neurosurgery, Endocrinology, Internal Medicine, Obstetrics, and Pediatrics
- lectured to community organizations and groups on topics of stress, relaxation, biofeedback, and pain management
- conducted in-service training for nurses and physicians
- guest lectured, Colleges of Medicine and Nursing

9/YR-24 – 8/YR-23   University of Nebraska Medical Center
Omaha, Nebraska (APA Approved)

Predoctoral Internship in Clinical Psychology

Teaching Experience:

YR-20 Central Nita Business School
Summerdale, Nita

Part-time Instructor in Psychology
- taught Psychology of the Physically Handicapped

YR-23 – YR-22   Buena Vista College
Council Bluffs, Iowa

Part-time Instructor in Psychology
- taught special topic seminar, social psychology, and Introduction to counseling to upper-level college students

3/YR-24 – 6/YR-24   The University of Health Sciences/The Chicago Medical School
North Chicago, Illinois

Child Cognitive Assessment Course (Graduate Level)
- supervised training in test administration
- lectured to students
- prepared and graded written and practical exams

Papers and Presentations:

Collins, L. (YR-5 May). *Ethics In Dealing With Disability Claims*, THE NITA PSYCHOLOGIST QUARTERLY, 62, 5, 8-9.

Collins, L. (YR-7, April.) *Long-term outcome in a chronic pain rehabilitation program.* Sixth World Congress on Pain, Adelaide, Australia

Wenner, E.J. & Collins, L. (YR-8, May). *Clinical efficacy of an interdisciplinary rehabilitation program for myofascial pain: an outcome study* First International Symposium on Myofascial Pain and Fibromyalgia, Minneapolis, Minnesota.

Collins, L. (YR-10). *Getting Injured Workers Back on the Job.* BUSINESS MONTH 4, 25.

Collins, L. (YR-12). *Work Related Injuries: Who Pays?* BUSINESS MONTH 3, 3, 10-13.

Guck, T.P.; Meilmann, P.S.; Skultety, F.M. & Collins, L. (YR-14). *Pain-Patient Minnesota Multiphasic Personality Inventory (MMPI) Subgroups: Evaluation of Long-Term Treatment Outcome.* JOURNAL OF BEHAVIORAL MEDICINE 11, 2, 159-169.

Collins, L. & Easterday, L. (YR-16, June). Chronic Benign Pain Rehabilitation and Return to Work: An Analysis of Behavioral Incentives. In *Employees: The Return to Work.* Symposium conducted at the annual meeting of the National Association of Rehabilitation Facilities, Seattle, Washington.

Collins, L. (YR-21). *Partner Weight and Relationship Style as Variable in Weight Reduction Treatment.* Unpublished doctoral thesis, University of Health Sciences/The Chicago Medical School, Chicago, Illinois.

Collins, L. & Black, D.R. (YR-23, August). A Review of Couples Interventions for Weight Loss. In D.F. Black (Chair) *Partners in Health Promotion: Another Look at Couples Intervention Programs.* Symposium conducted at the American Psychological Association, Toronto, Canada.

Black, D.R. & Collins, L. (YR-23, July). Self-Monitoring of Feelings and Emotions as a Module in a Communications Skills Course. Paper presented at the Annual Meetings of the American Association of College of Pharmacy, Baltimore, Maryland.

Memberships:
American Psychological Association
Association for the Advancement of Psychology
Pennsylvania Psychological Association
     Insurance Committee YR-13 – Present
     (Committee Chair, YR-11 – YR-9)
     Membership Committee YR-10 – Present
     Ethics Committee YR-9 – Present
NitaPsy PAC Board Member (YR-8 – Present)
International Association for the Study of Pain
American Pain Society
Society for Behavioral Medicine
Society of Chronic Pain Management, Board Member (YR-19 – YR-9)
Nita County Committee on Employment of People with Disabilities,
     President YR-18 – YR-17

December 15, YR-1

David Payton, Esq.
Payton and Payton
P.O. Box 1976
3513 North Front Street
Nita City, Nita 09102

Dear Mr. Payton:

I am a specialist in psychiatry, licensed in the State of Nita. I am currently employed by the Lancaster General Hospital System as vice president in charge of behavioral health services, which involves supervision of the psychiatrists for both inpatient and outpatient care. I also supervise approximately one hundred physicians employed by the Lancaster General Hospital System. I do not treat patients in these supervisory capacities.

In addition, I have a part-time forensic practice making evaluations such as the one I performed on Trooper Stucky. I perform on average four evaluations a month. I am qualified as an expert witness in the United States District Court for the Eastern, Middle, and Western Districts of Nita; federal court in Alexandria, Virginia; and in courts of common pleas throughout the State of Nita. I charge $350 per hour for out-of-court work and $450 per hour for time testifying in court.

In my practice, I have treated several individuals with posttraumatic stress disorder (PTSD). I treated two individuals in particular on a weekly basis for well over ten years. One individual, a veteran of the Vietnam War, was a medic who had witnessed several friends killed. The other individual was a woman who was being physically and sexually abused by her husband, and had a family history of sexual abuse. I have evaluated several other patients with PTSD and have treated patients with PTSD on a short-term basis.

Your office requested that I conduct an independent psychiatric evaluation of Clayton Stucky. An objective, independent psychiatric evaluation differs from treatment by a psychiatrist or psychologist. In the latter instance, the professional's role is to listen to the patient's report of symptoms, to understand what they are going through, and to provide the course of treatment. It is generally not the role of the treater to critically evaluate the validity of what the patient is saying. In particular, it is not the role of the treating psychiatrist to question whether the individual may be malingering or exaggerating symptoms in order for some secondary purpose, such as monetary gain. So the treating psychiatrist listens, and empathizes, while the patient generally sets the tone of the session, directing the discussion. As an independent evaluator, it is my role to take more of a critical look at what is reported, to look for inconsistencies, to see if symptoms reported meet specific criteria for diagnosis and whether what the patient is saying really holds true. The fact that I am retained or paid for an evaluation does not have any effect on the way I conduct the evaluation or the opinions I reach. My credibility and reputation as a psychiatrist rest on the fact that many times I do not come up with favorable opinions for the people who are paying me to conduct the evaluation.

In particular, you asked me to determine whether Mr. Stucky had, or continues to suffer from, PTSD. I spent six or seven hours reviewing the records of Dr. Stovall and Dr. Collins. I also saw Mr. Stucky in my office on October 25, YR-1 for approximately seventy minutes and performed a diagnostic evaluation. Mr. Stucky arrived alone and on time. I explained the limits of the confidentiality of the evaluation: that I would share my report and evaluation with the attorneys and the court. As with every evaluation, I obtained a thorough medical history from Mr. Stucky, because certain medical conditions can contribute to psychiatric symptoms. I obtained a thorough psychosocial history, looking for anything that might be pertinent to the current symptomology. I also performed a formal mental status exam, which is the psychological equivalent to a medical doctor's physical exam. I observed how Mr. Stucky related to me throughout the interview.

I asked Mr. Stucky to describe the event and his response to it, his subsequent reaction, the treatment he received following the event, and how he responded to that treatment. Mr. Stucky expressed considerable anger at being pulled over by the police, feeling that it happened because of his race. He repeated many times that Officers Conlee and Parsell had lied, and that throughout this process they had not conducted themselves in a manner consistent with how he would act as a state trooper. He indicated that he became preoccupied with the incident, that it was very difficult for him to concentrate at work, that he would spend a large amount of time reviewing what the defendants in this suit had said.

Mr. Stucky's primary response to the incident was anger, and he also described having severe headaches that awakened him in the middle of the night. He told me that he had not had problems with headaches prior to this incident and that he had no psychiatric or psychological treatment prior to this incident. His medical records, however, indicate a prior history of migraine headaches.

Mr. Stucky said that at some point he came to peace with himself, largely through remembering what his grandmother, now deceased, had told him. His grandmother's advice had to do with religion, relying upon God as a way of letting some of this go.

What is remarkable is that Mr. Stucky was very calm throughout the evaluation. He did not show any kind of discomfort or agitation. He could talk about this episode without hesitation. Though he expressed anger, he appeared very controlled and carefully measured his answers. He evaded some questions, and even though I repeated them several times he would not give me a direct answer. I therefore believe that he was not being completely forthright.

When diagnosing a patient, the standard method is an analysis of five axes. Axis one is a description of any acute psychiatric or psychological disorder. My conclusion is that Mr. Stucky did not suffer any major psychiatric disorder at this time, and did not meet the criteria of any axis one diagnosis.

Axis two is a description or diagnosis of the person's underlying personality. Mr. Stucky exhibited symptoms of long-standing anger issues, impacting his response to the traffic stop. My opinion is that he has an uncategorized personality disorder. My opinion is based upon his reaction to this evaluation. While it is understandable that a plaintiff would feel defensive in the situation, Mr. Stucky's angry and uncooperative reaction went beyond the reaction I generally see in similar situations. He displayed controlled passive aggressive traits. He expressed his anger by indirect means: he was evasive; he obstructed the process; he passively withheld cooperation. He exhibited some classic narcissistic traits. He was aloof, showing very little emotion aside from the anger described. It was difficult to connect with him, above and beyond what I normally see in such evaluations. He presented moments of arrogance and the sense that he deserved special treatment; this was revealed in particular when he talked about the incident.

Personality disorders tend to present early in a person's life and they tend to be relatively stable. I inquired about past events that may have contributed to his anger. He minimized certain events in his life that clearly would incite anger, such as his contentious divorce and custody battle. He also talked briefly about the fact that his father was absent from his life. These are events that usually have a substantial impact on people, and he denied that.

Axis three is an evaluation of any medical or psychological conditions. His history of migraine headaches fulfills this axis.

Axis four is a description of current stressors, and a major stressor in his life at this point, in my opinion, is his legal difficulties. I did not note any other current stressors at the time of the evaluation.

The fifth axis identifies the person's level of function on a scale of 0 to 100. Because of the brief time I spent with Mr. Stucky, I can only give a gross estimate of functionality as compared to a fully functioning person. I judged him to be fully functioning by the time that I saw him.

I also performed a mental status evaluation, consisting of how he related to me, how much affect—which is emotional expression—he displayed, his mood, whether he showed any signs of neurological or organic impairment. His mental status was unremarkable except for what I described before as aloofness and lack of emotion apart from anger. He presented no evidence of psychotic symptoms such as hallucinations or delusions. He was not suicidal and was not expressing any homicidal ideation.

I saw no evidence that he currently suffers posttraumatic stress disorder, and it is it my opinion to a reasonable degree of medical certainty that Mr. Stucky exhibited no signs or symptoms indicating that he had PTSD previously. PTSD requires the individual to have experienced an actual or threatened severe threat; PTSD sufferers respond with characteristic development of symptoms, including extreme fear, helplessness, or horror. In my opinion, the incident in question did not come close to rising to the level of severity to produce PTSD. Neither Officer Conlee nor Officer Parsell drew his gun or verbally threatened to shoot Mr. Stucky or Ms. Elliot. The examples of traumatic events listed in the "Diagnostic Features" section of the DSM-5 regarding PTSD—such as exposure to war, childhood physical abuse, sexual trafficking, and terrorist attack—are a far cry from a routine traffic stop for a speeding violation. Mr. Stucky would be less likely than the average citizen to be traumatized by a traffic stop. Not only has he experienced these stops on a daily basis in his work; as a police officer, he would understand that the greatest danger in a traffic stop is to the officer. Stucky would and should have comprehended how his aberrant and noncompliant behavior would cause

Officers Conlee and Parsell concern for their own safety, and Stucky could and should have viewed their behavior through that lens.

The primary response to a perceived threat of actual harm is one of intense fear or horror or helplessness, and Mr. Stucky did not describe having any of these feelings. Mr. Stucky's use of his cell phone to call his supervisor indicates that he was thinking rationally at the time and was attempting to influence the situation.

While by no means endorsing or diminishing the effect of racial discrimination on persons of color, even if we were to assume that Stucky was stopped because of his race, it would not have caused PTSD. I imagine Stucky suffered more discrimination at the hands of motorists he stopped and from the Nita State Police hierarchy than any feeling of being wronged that could have flowed from this traffic stop. If a diagnosis that Stucky suffered from PTSD were valid, the entire American populace of color could bring the same claim simply by virtue of being a minority member living in a white power structure. Frankly, Mr. Stucky's claim of PTSD diminishes and demeans those social and political movements fighting for equality.

According to Dr. Collins's notes, much of his therapy seemed to be directed towards Trooper Stucky's response to the stress of hearings, the stress of reviewing information arising from his lawsuit. This course of therapy is not unusual—in fact, I would characterize it as expected, under the circumstances. But the stress from events subsequent to the traffic stop would not contribute to a diagnosis of PTSD as a result of the incident. I also note that in December of YR-2, Dr. Stovall, Mr. Stucky's family physician, prescribed Imitrex for Mr. Stucky's migraine headaches. Imitrex is a beta blocker primarily is used to treat high blood pressure, but is also prescribed for the prevention of migraine headaches. Unfortunately, clinical depression is a known side effect in about two-thirds of the individuals who take Imitrex, and Dr. Stovall's notes indicate that shortly after prescribing Imitrex she received a call from Trooper Stucky's fiancée expressing concern about his condition. This is when he referred Mr. Stucky to Dr. Collins. The medication quite likely contributed to what Dr. Collins saw or heard about in March of YR-1.

Very truly yours,

/s/ *Jeremiah Guttman*
Jeremiah Guttman, MD
Guttman Forensics LLC

CURRICULUM VITAE
DR. JEREMIAH GUTTMAN

Employment

YR-3 to present
    Vice President, Behavioral Health Service
    Lancaster General Hospital System
    Lancaster, Nita

YR-12 to present
    CEO and Owner
    Guttman Forensics LLC
    Independent Medical Examiner

YR-28 to YR-3
    Private Practice
    Guttman and Associates

Education

YR-36
    BA Washington, College
    St. Louis, Missouri

YR-32
    MD Georgetown University Medical Center
    Washington, D.C.

YR-28 through YR-32
    Psychiatric Residency
    Georgetown University

Honors

Distinguished Fellow of the American
Psychiatric Association (awarded to less than 5 percent of psychiatrists in the
country)

Certifications

Board Certified in Psychiatry (YR-25)
Active Licensure: Nita
Inactive Licensure: District of Columbia, Maryland, Virginia

Memberships

American Psychiatric Association
American Academy of Psychiatry and Law
American Medical Association
Lancaster County Medical Society

Teaching

Assistant Professor of Psychiatry, Georgetown University
Assistant Professor of Psychiatry, Nita University

Publications   *Managing Psychiatrists within Hospital Systems: Challenges and Opportunities for the Administrator,* JOURNAL OF THE ASSOCIATION OF AMERICAN HOSPITALS, January YR-2

Independent Evaluation versus Treatment: The Role And Ethical Responsibilities of the Psychiatrist in Disparate Settings, JOURNAL OF THE AMERICAN PSYCHIATRIC ASSOCIATION, April YR-4

Using Medical History to Aid in Diagnosing Long-term Personality Disorders, JOURNAL OF THE AMERICA MEDICAL ASSOCIATION, September YR-15

Enhancing Axis Two Diagnoses, JOURNAL OF THE AMERICAN ACADEMY OF PSYCHIATRY AND LAW, June YR-20

EXHIBITS

Exhibit 1

Photo of Stucky's vehicle

Note: Color copies of all exhibits can be found at the following website:

http://bit.ly/1P20Jea
Password: Stucky2

Exhibit 2

Google Maps diagram map of the East Market Street area

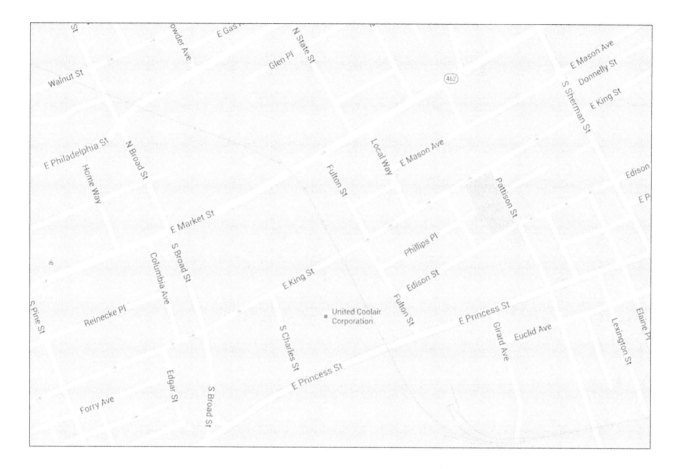

Exhibit 3

Google Earth overhead map of East Market Street area

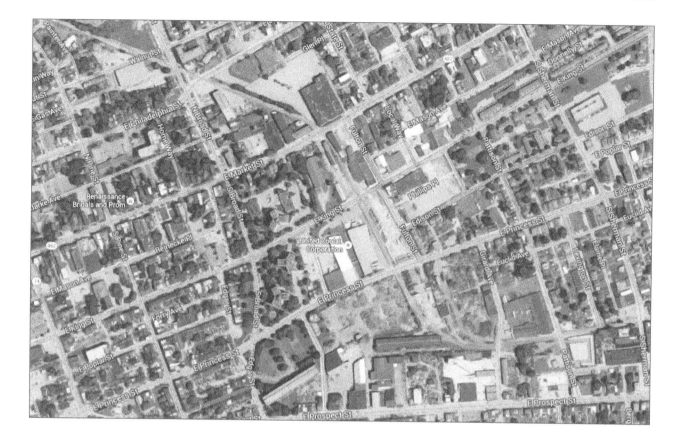

Exhibit 4

Google Earth street view map of railroad tracks on East Market Street

Exhibit 5

Street view photo of East Market Street, looking West from where Stucky was stopped

Exhibit 6

Street view of East Market Street where Stucky was stopped

Exhibit 7

Close-up street view of East Market Street where Stucky was stopped

Exhibit 8

Photo of door showing address at point of stop

Exhibit 9

STATE OF NITA

TRAFFIC CITATION

CITATION NO.
A7190100-1

| 1. Magisterial District No. 19-01-01 | | 2. Docket Number |

3. Address of Magisterial District Officer
204 E. King St Nita City, Nita

| 4. Driver Number 12-019-497 | 5. C.D.L. ☐ | 6. State. ☑ NITA | 7. D.O.B. 3/22/yr-34 | 8. Sex ☑ M ☐ F |

9. Defendant Name - First   Middle   Last
Clayton   Stucky

10. Defendant Address (Street-City-State-Zip Code)
179 Laurel Lane   Nita City, Nita

| 11. Veh. Reg. No. EN PA2 | 12. Reg. Yr. Yr-2 | 13. State ☑ NITA | 14. Make Lexus | 15. Type Sdn | 16. Color Tan |
| 17. Veh. Reg. No. | 18. Reg. Yr. | 19. State ☐ NITA | 20. Make | 21. Type | 22. Color |

22. Owner/License or Carrier Name & Address   ☐ Same as Defendant   ☐ Not Required
Same as above

24. Charge
☐ Maximum Speed-Limits
☐ Stop Signs & Yield Signs
☑ Driving Vehicle at Unsafe Speed
☐ Operation of Vehicle without Official Certificate of Inspection
☐ Driving while Operating Privilege is suspended/Revoked License
☐ Other _____
☐ Drivers Required to be Licensed
☐ Registration & Certification of Title Required
☐ Unlawful Activities
☐ Careless Driving
☐ Traffic-Control Signals

26 ☐ STATUE Title 75 ☐ ORDINANCE	
27. SEC 3361	28. SUB SEC
29. FINE 25.00	
30. EMS 10.00	
31. CAT 30.00	
32. COSTS 24.00	
33. JCP 10.60	
34. TOTAL DUE $104.60	

25. Nature of Offense
☐ Speeding ___ MPH Allowed ___ MPH
☐ Operated Vehicle with Expired Inspection
☐ Operated Vehicle with Suspended/Revoked License
☐ Violated 67 Nita Code ___   Ref. 49 CNA
☐ Radar ☐ Clocked ☐ A.O.V.
☐ ESP ☐ Vascar ☐ Other
☐ Operated Vehicle without Valid License
☐ Operated Unregistered Vehicle

☑ Other Said defendant did drive a
vehicle that was neither reasonable or prudent
for the road conditions. Rain-wet roadway
speed in excess of 60 mph

☐ Filed on Info Received

35. Location East Market Street 700 block		36. Zone
37. Route 462	38. Twp-Boro-City Nita	39. Code 201	40. Dir. of Travel N S E W
41. Date 8/5/Yr-2	42. Time 1150	43. Day Tue	44. County Nita	45. Code 67

46. Defendants Signature refused to sign   47. Date Issued 8/5/Yr-2

48. I verify that the set facts in this citation are true and correct to the best of my knowledge, information and belief.
Eric Conlee   badge # 12-130

49. Section Address of Police Officer
28 East Market Street Nita City, Nita   50. ORJ Number 067000

51. Speed Timing Device Operator	52. Miles Followed	53. Miles Timed	54. Secs. Timed
55. Speed Equip. Serial No. N/A	56. Station Equip. Tested N/A	57. Date Equip. Tested
58. Accident Report No.	59. 75Na. CSA 11545 Violation Parents Notified ☐ Yes ☐ No	60. Comm. Veh. ☐ Yes	61. Haz. Mar. ☐ Yes

62. Remarks
Officer Lance Parsell
City of Nita Police Dept

NOTICE

If you plead guilty or are not found guilty, points may be assessed against your driver's record. Accumulation of 11 or more points will result in the suspension of your driving privilege. Also, your driving privilege WILL BE SUSPENDED if you plead guilty or are found guilty of certain offenses under the Vehicle Code, Including but not limited to driving while operating privilge is suspended or revoked, racing on highways, fleeing or attempting to elude police, driving without lights to avoid identification or arrest, accidents involving damage to attending vehicles or property, failure to stop for school bus with flashing lights, or subsequent convictions related to drivers required to be licensed.

AOPC 406-95 (REV, 1/2000)   **DISTRICT JUSTICE**   **A7190100-1**

Exhibit 10

IN THE CITY OF NITA CITY
MUNICIPAL COURT

NITA CITY	:	JUDGE HELEN L. DALEY
	:	
v.	:	TR-2479
	:	
CLAYTON STUCKY	:	TRANSCRIPT OF PROCEEDINGS
	:	PRELIMINARY HEARING

DATE: NOVEMBER 5, YR-2, 10:00 A.M.

PLACE: 204 EAST KING STREET

                NITA CITY, NITA

APPEARANCES:

NITA CITY POLICE DEPARTMENT

BY: ERIC CONLEE AND LANCE PARSELL

         FOR – STATE OF NITA

LAW OFFICE OF CLINTON T. MANGES

BY: CLINTON T. MANGES, ESQUIRE

         FOR – DEFENDANT

PATSY A. SITWELL, REPORTER

NOTARY PUBLIC

THE COURT: This is the City of Nita City vs. Clayton Stucky, Docket TR-2479 of YR-2.

Call your first witness.

OFFICER CONLEE: Your Honor, I'll testify myself, and Officer Parsell will also be testifying

for the City.

MR. MANGES: Your Honor, we'd request respectfully that the second witness be sequestered then.

THE COURT: OK. Step outside, please.

ERIC CONLEE, called as a witness, being sworn, testified as follows:

DIRECT TESTIMONY

OFFICE CONLEE: Your Honor, I'm Officer Eric L. Conlee. I'm a member of the Nita City Police Department. I was so employed, I was in full uniform, and I was operating a marked Nita City Police Department vehicle on the date of the violation, which was the fifth of August YR-2. This offense occurred on or about 11:50 a.m. It occurred on East Market Street, general vicinity 700 block of East Market Street eastbound.

Your Honor, before I actually go into my testimony, I would like to testify as to my training and how I could calculate speed based on my years of experience. I would ask the Court to indulge me a little bit on that.

I've been in law enforcement for about thirty-five years. I was a police officer with Nita Township for thirty-one years, and during the course of those thirty-one years I had been involved in using numerous speed timing devices. They include the basic calibrated stopwatch; ESP, which is a traffic control device; Accutrack (phonetic); and also VASCAR (phonetic). All of these devices in some way, shape, or form involved, either in setting them up or observing traffic, my personally estimating the speed of a particular vehicle. In the course of my career, I have stopped tens of thousands of cars, and made numerous traffic arrests based on my knowledge and estimate of speed.

I'm a graduate of the Nita State Police Academy, where I was trained by Nita State Police. I'm also a graduate of the Traffic Institute out at Northwestern University, which I attended on two different occasions. I also received the Governor's Traffic Award for traffic enforcement. I have

attended many, many seminars and schools which have to do with traffic enforcement. I have trained

and instructed members of the district attorney's office on traffic. I was the coordinator and I was the

training instructor for Nita Township, were I worked for many years. I also ran their field training

program, which includes traffic training. I'm currently the traffic enforcement training officer for the

Nita City Police Department.

What I'm trying to say here basically is that I have a vast knowledge in estimating speed, and

I believe that if it would be possible to consider yourself an expert in this area that I feel I—

MR. MANGES: I'll object to any reference to—

OFFICER CONLEE: It's my opinion that I'm an expert in this area.

MR. MANGES: An expert would require specific instruction. Speed is specifically, by law, an

area that remains a lay opinion, and hence, I would object to any attempt to characterize a lay opinion

as expert.

OFFICER CONLEE: Your Honor, this is his opinion. If he can show me something in writing

to this effect—I have testified in court many times. I have had judges—

MR. MANGES: How about we do it this way: he's offered himself as an expert. May I

voir dire?

THE COURT: Go right ahead.

CROSS-EXAMINATION AS TO QUALIFICATIONS

BY MR. MANGES:

Q. Can you name one recorded court case where you have been qualified by a court of

   common pleas as an expert witness?

A. I can only tell you that—no, no.

Q. Essentially, each of those courses that you took—Accutrack, VASCAR, all of those speed timing stopwatch devices—were in order to establish that you could establish a maximum speed based upon the reading of the clock, correct?

A. Not in all cases, no. A lot of them have to do with your actual—your visual look at the vehicle. The ultimate result would be based on the distance and the time, correct.

Q. Correct. I mean that's—

A. But still I had to estimate the speed in my own mind to decide whether to clock that car or not. I would say, oh, this vehicle here is going at such and such a speed, I'm going to clock that vehicle. Some of the devices, that's the technique I would use.

Q. That would be your decision. But as far as establishing speed, it was the use of the approved equipment, the traffic control device, that allowed you to render a speed.

A. Sure. You needed the actual—that's correct.

Q. Thank you. And, as a matter of fact, the courses you've described, none of those courses basically trained you to actually estimate a speed with any scientific specificity, correct?

A. That's not true. If you use a stopwatch, you have to sit there and you have to visibly see a vehicle. I don't remember verbatim the exact training guidelines, but you need some degree of certainty that you think a vehicle is going at a particular speed.

Q. In order to give you essentially a reasonable suspicion in order to activate the timing device, correct?

A. That's correct.

Q. But none of those courses train you to specifically estimate a speed with scientific certainty, correct?

A. But, remarkably, when the speed is exposed it's—most of the time, that's the speed I felt it was going to be before the actual clock so—

Q. That's what you felt.

A. Yeah, based on all my training and all my years.

Q. But no course ever trained you specifically—

A. I'll leave that up to the courts.

Q. I'd like you to answer the question. Have you ever been trained specifically to estimate a speed on your own, without the equipment, to scientific certainty?

A. I don't think there are any courses which do that.

MR. MANGES: I have no further questions.

THE COURT: OK.

OFFICER CONLEE: Now, Your Honor, I would like to go into my actual testimony.

THE COURT: OK.

DIRECT TESTIMONY

OFFICER CONLEE: On this particular date and time I was involved in traffic enforcement training. I had another officer with me. I was operating, like I said, a marked Nita City Police Department vehicle, and we were en route to an area that I had designated for our training. Our course took us on East Market Street, eastbound, as it is a one-way street. I was in the left lane. I was the operator of the vehicle, and the other officer was in the right front seat.

At the time we were traveling on Market Street, it was raining. The roadways were very wet, and it was raining I'd say light to moderate at the time. The particular area on Market Street is a twenty-five-mile-an-hour speed zone. To the best of my knowledge, this twenty-five-mile-an-hour speed zone runs—starts on the west side of Nita City and extends on out into the Spring Garden section of the city. As I was traveling in the left eastbound lane—I do not have a calibrated speed timing device or speedometer in my vehicle but the speedometer that I—

MR. MANGES: I object to any reference to a speedometer if it's not calibrated.

THE COURT: Sustained.

OFFICER CONLEE: I was traveling, in my opinion, about twenty-five miles an hour. A vehicle traveling in the right eastbound lane coming from my right rear passed my vehicle at a high rate of speed. I estimate that that vehicle was traveling between fifty, fifty-five miles an hour.

At this time I determined that this vehicle was traveling at a speed which I believed to be in excess of fifty miles an hour. Of course, it was raining, the roadways were wet. I made a determination that I was going to stop the vehicle for driving a vehicle at an unsafe speed. And, incidentally, the particular area where this particular vehicle had passed through included one intersection, which was Fulton Street, and there's another intersection that would have been—but I know for a fact that it had crossed one intersection. This particular area is—it's a residential and it's a business district. It has some businesses, and it has some homes. There are cars parked on both sides of the road. There were people on the road or on the sidewalks, but how many I don't know.

I activated my emergency lights—the vehicle has a standard rooftop bar light, which is red and blue, and we have other different type of lights. I put all the lights on for the purpose of stopping this particular vehicle, which turned out to be a Lexus sedan, Nita Registration ENPAZ. I stopped this vehicle on the—up against the left curb of East Market Street. I parked directly behind.

The defendant, Mr. Stucky, was driving, and a woman sat in the front passenger seat. I don't know exactly what her age was.

We made contact with Control to let them know where we were, the type of vehicle, the cause of the stop, and all the other circumstances that have to do with a basic traffic stop. I exited the patrol vehicle and walked to the driver's side door of the Lexus. I asked the operator for his driver's license and his registration card. The operator at that point reached over and picked up a cell phone, making no attempt to exhibit his driver's license or registration card. I waited a few seconds then said, "Sir, I would like to see your driver's license and registration." The man acted as if I wasn't even there.

He started talking to somebody on the cell phone. At that time I, again, asked him for his driver's license and registration. Again, I was totally ignored. This went on several more times. At some point, he laid the phone down, and I believe it was probably an open line on the phone so the person on the other end could hear the conversation. After numerous requests for him to give me his identification, he finally got out his driver's license and his registration card.

Mr. Stucky never mentioned where he worked, or his occupation. I advised him that he had been driving approximately fifty, fifty-five miles an hour in a twenty-five-mile-per-hour speed limit zone. He told me he didn't feel he was going that fast, but I said that, based on the weather conditions, the area, the fact that the roadway was wet, I was ticketing him for driving a vehicle at an unsafe speed under Section 3361.

I then asked Mr. Stucky if I could search a bag in the rear seat of his car.

MR. MANGES: Objection. Any reference to request to a search after the stop is irrelevant to whether Mr. Stucky violated the Motor Vehicle Code, which is the only issue before this Court.

THE COURT: Sustained

OFFICER CONLEE: I went back to the patrol car and requested a license check from Nita City Control.

While I was writing up the citation for driving a vehicle at an unsafe speed, I received a call from the Nita City Police Department dispatch. Chief Lieber wanted to see us about our stopping a state trooper.

I completed the traffic citation, got out of my vehicle. I walked back up to the driver's window and explained the violation to Mr. Stucky. I asked him if he wanted to sign the citation, and he told me no. He then asked me I needed anything else. I said no, and he drove off.

Based on all the circumstances, there is absolutely no doubt in my mind that the defendant was traveling well in excess of the posted speed limit; and, based on the conditions, there is absolutely no doubt in my mind that he committed the violation for which I ticketed him.

CROSS-EXAMINATION

BY MR. MANGES:

Q. I notice on the citation where you allege the violations would be in the 700 block of East Market Street, correct?

A. That's correct.

Q. And you indicate that you were traveling eastbound, is that correct?

A. That's correct.

Q. And the 700 block would be delineated by which two streets?

A. I'm not that well—I'm not sure if it's Fulton and—I don't know all the streets of the city. I don't—to tell you the truth, I'm not sure.

Q. OK. It was in that block between Fulton and—

A. If you listened to my testimony, that's the point that he went by my vehicle. We're traveling down the road. We're certainly covering a little bit more—that's the general vicinity but that's the point where he accelerated by my vehicle.

Q. There's a traffic signal at Broad Street, correct?

A. Broad Street?

Q. Or is that Pine Street?

A. I'm not sure. You're probably—one of them I think there is.

Q. OK. And isn't it correct that both your vehicle and his vehicle were stopped at that red light?

A. Yes.

Q. Where was Mr. Stucky in relation to your vehicle when you first observed him driving, sir?

A. In the opposite lane.

Q. Next to your vehicle?

A. Coming up from our rear.

Q. How far back?

A. I don't know. It just was a blur going by. I looked out the right side of the vehicle, and there was this vehicle accelerating by us at a high rate of speed. I would say we were crossing through an intersection, but we were never at a stop.

Q. And at what point—was it still on that block when you activated your lights?

A. I believe that's where the actual—the lights actually went on I think in the 700, but I'm not 100 percent sure as far as the exact spot where I put the lights on because you have reaction time and everything else to take into consideration, but it was that general vicinity.

Q. So it's fair to assume then that as soon as you made the observation, you activated your lights and then pursued the vehicle, correct?

A. Well, within a reasonable amount of time as far as my reaction goes.

Q. OK. Did he change lanes in front of you?

A. Pardon?

Q. Did he change lanes?

A. When he saw the lights, he moved into the left eastbound lane. He had to do that in order to get to the left curb.

Q. OK. Which is where he went?

A. Yes.

Q. And you went back—you were behind him in the right lane, and then you went back to the left lane behind him, is that correct?

A. No. I was always in the left lane.

Q. You never got behind him?

A. I'm in the left lane, he's in the right lane. He passes me, my lights come on, he moves to the left lane and pulls up to the curb. I never changed lanes. He does.

Q. After you activated your lights, how quickly did he pull over?

A. Hit the brakes, slowed down real fast, pulled over to the left-hand curb, just like a reaction type thing.

Q. So there was an immediate response to your lights?

A. Yes.

Q. Is it fair to assume that you would have called in the traffic stop before getting out of your car and approaching his?

A. I would say yes.

Q. And did you approach alone or—

A. Initially I approached alone, and then my partner came up.

Q. Do you recall at what point in this transaction that your partner—or trainee I guess it would be—approached?

A. Probably within a—I wouldn't think more than say a minute would have lapsed.

Q. And when you expressed that you believed he was going in excess of fifty miles per hour, he asserted that he was not going that fast, correct?

A. He made a comment to the effect that, no, I wasn't going that fast.

Q. At that point did he ask you what clocking device you used?

A. No.

Q. Was there a conversation?

A. That was the last words out of his mouth, and then he went into the cell phone thing. That's the last comment he made to me.

Q. At any point did you observe his vehicle in unsafe proximity to any other vehicle on the roadway?

A. Just our vehicle and his. Nobody in the immediate area, except for vehicles parked on the sides of the road.

Q. But at no point did he appear to be out of control or moving towards those vehicles in an unusual manner?

A. I thought he was out of control by the speed he was driving.

Q. I understand your opinion as to his speed, but I'm talking about anything else to indicate that he was moving closely to those parked vehicles on the side.

A. No, no. He was going straight, probably centered in his lane.

Q. The area that you were talking about, is that one of those areas that you're aware of is a drug area?

A. I have no idea. You mean like marijuana or are you talking about —

Q. I often times hear officers testify to areas known as drug areas versus other areas. Is there any special—

A. I don't get involved in that.

Q. The fact that he was driving a Lexus, would that have anything to do with your decision to stop him?

A. No. I didn't—I wasn't even aware of that until—I'm not real good as far as—I don't see cars and know that they're particular models. I knew it was a larger vehicle.

Q. Did you make any other observations of the operator of the vehicle prior to stopping it?

A. No. It was—kind of had that misty/foggy type thing, and the windows were wet. I had no idea who was in the vehicle.

Q. Did you make—

A. Or how nice the car was or anything like that, no.

Q. Did you make any observation of how he might have been seated in the vehicle, whether he was wearing a hat or anything else prior to your making the traffic stop?

A. No. All I saw was a vehicle go by fast, and I stopped it. I didn't see anything until I walked up to the car. I didn't care who was in the car.

Q. Is it fair to say from the time—the place where you first observed the vehicle to the place where you stopped the vehicle would be about one-tenth of a mile, correct?

A. I first observed him—no. I don't know. One-tenth, that's 500 and some feet, so probably further than that. Maybe two-tenths, three-tenths of a mile. I don't know.

Q. Clearly, less than three-tenths of a mile, correct?

A. I gave you three-tenths, yeah. I'd say that's probably—

Q. Less than three?

A. —the minimum, yeah.

Q. And, again, there was no attempt on your part to do a pace mode tracking or anything else, is that correct?

A. I didn't have any speed timing devices in the vehicle.

Q. Well, didn't you say that you were training someone in traffic?

A. That day the training was just about general traffic, stop signs, red lights, inspections. We had no speed timing device in the vehicle.

Q. Isn't that something you would normally train someone on, the traffic division of the—

A. Not that day—it was the first day of on-the-road training.

THE COURT: Anything further?

OFFICER CONLEE: No, Your Honor.

THE COURT: You may step down.

THE COURT: Call your next witness.

OFFICER CONLEE: Lance Parsell.

LANCE PARSELL, called as a witness, being sworn, testified as follows:

DIRECT EXAMINATION

BY OFFICER CONLEE:

Q. Officer Parsell, would you tell the Court what your name is, where you work, and how long you've been employed?

A. Lance S. Parsell, P-A-R-S-E-L-L. I work for the Nita City Police Department. I've been there about three years.

Q. On the fifth of August YR-2, would you tell the Court exactly what your duties were on that particular date and what you were involved in?

A. On that date, we were involved in some traffic training that we were doing—selective traffic enforcement throughout Nita City.

Q. And who were you being trained by?

A. Yourself, Officer Conlee.

Q. On that particular date, did we have an occasion to be on East Market Street?

A. Yes.

Q. Would you tell the Court exactly where you were, the direction of travel, the approximate time, and some of the other circumstances as far as our movement went.

A. At approximately 11:50 a.m. in the morning, we were eastbound on East Market Street, approximately the 300 block. We were in the left-hand lane.

Q. And what direction were we traveling?

A. East.

Q. OK. And would you tell the Court in your own words exactly what occurred as we were traveling east on East Market Street.

A. A brown or tan Lexus drove by us at a high rate of speed. We were in the left-hand lane. The vehicle was in the right-hand lane.

Q. OK. When the vehicle actually passed our vehicle, where in proximity to some reference point off of Market Street would we have been?

A. I'd say it was approximately the 300 to 400 block.

Q. Do you have any idea what speed that particular vehicle was driving at that time? Do you have an opinion?

A. Approximately fifty to fifty-five miles per hour.

Q. And what are you basing that opinion on?

A. I was basing that on the fact that we were driving approximately twenty-five miles per hour. The vehicle passed at a high rate of speed, and we had to accelerate to at least that point to catch the vehicle.

Q. About how much time elapsed from the time that we first saw the vehicle until the emergency lights were activated?

A. After the vehicle passed us, it wasn't much time. You indicated that the vehicle had gone by us at a high rate of speed and that was a good example of—

Q. Would you say it was fairly immediate?

A. Yes.

Q. Could you tell when the vehicle was traveling past who was driving that vehicle?

A. I could only see it was a male driver at that time.

Q. OK. You couldn't—could you tell whether that person was black, white, wearing a hat, or could you see any other—what he was wearing or anything like that?

A.   Not at that time when he went by. It was quick. I just knew it was a black male driver.

Q.   What did that vehicle do when we activated the emergency lights?

A.   It pulled over to the left-hand side of East Market Street in approximately the 700 block.

Q.   And was I, in fact, the operator of the Nita City Police Department vehicle?

A.   Yes.

Q.   Where did I position my vehicle in relation to that particular vehicle?

A.   You positioned it behind his vehicle.

Q.   Who actually contacted Nita City Control to let them know that we had made the traffic stop?

A.   I did.

Q.   Who got out of the Nita City Police Department vehicle first?

A.   You did.

Q.   And what did I do?

A.   You approached the driver's side door.

Q.   And approximately how much time had elapsed before you got out and approached the vehicle, just guessing?

A.   Fifteen seconds at the most.

Q.   A relatively short time?

A.   Yes.

Q.   Where did you position yourself?

A. I positioned myself to the passenger's side, slightly behind the passenger's side door.

Q. Where on East Market Street were we actually stopped?

A. The 700 block past Fulton Street, I believe.

Q. Do you know what the distance is from the 300 block to the 700 block of East Market Street? I know we're talking four blocks, but do you know as far as part of a mile what — if you had to guesstimate, would that be a tenth of a mile, two-tenths, three-tenths? Are you 100 percent sure that — how did you know it was the 300 block and not the 400 or 500 block?

A. I'm estimating.

Q. But you don't really—you're not really sure?

A. No.

Q. When you first observed the vehicle, it could have been anywhere prior to the 700 block. You're not really 100 percent sure of that spot, right?

A. Correct.

Q. Did you have an occasion to hear any of the conversation that I had with the driver of that vehicle?

A. Not initially, but after I saw that it seemed like you were having a problem with the driver, I came around to reposition myself on the driver's side of the vehicle.

Q. Incidentally, is the driver of that vehicle in the courtroom today?

A. Yes, he is.

Q. Could you point him out, please?

A. He's sitting at the defense table next to counsel.

Q. OK. When you said I was having a problem with the driver, would you explain to the Court what you mean by that?

A. When I first observed you, it seemed like you were having trouble getting information from him. That's when I came around to your side of the vehicle, and that's when you were repeatedly asking him for his operator's license.

Q. Do you know approximately how many times you heard me ask him for his driver's license and registration card?

A. Approximately six or seven.

Q. During the time that I asked him for his driver's license and his registration card, was I polite?

A. Yes.

Q. Did I constantly refer to him as sir?

MR. MANGES: I'll object to the leading questions.

THE COURT: Sustained. They're leading.

BY OFFICER CONLEE:

Q. At what point did I actually receive the driver's license and registration card?

A. After several repeated requests for it, he did finally give it to you.

Q. At the time of this particular violation, would you tell the Court what the conditions were at that time.

A. It was a light rain. The roads were wet.

OFFICER CONLEE: I think that's it, Your Honor. No further questions.

THE COURT: OK.

CROSS-EXAMINATION

BY MR. MANGES:

Q. When the vehicle went by, did you have a conversation with your training officer as to what he observed?

A. Yes. Officer Conlee did say—

Q. He made a statement to you?

Q. He gave you an estimate as to what the speed was?

A. Yes, he did, and I concurred with that.

Q. And at that point you concurred with your training officer, correct?

A. Correct.

Q. And he then proceeded to follow the vehicle, correct?

A. Yes.

Q. At any point did you ever see that Lexus come close to striking any other vehicle on the roadway?

A. No.

Q. When he put on the emergency lights, you would be aware of that while you were in the passenger's seat of the squad car, correct?

A. Yes.

Q. How much time elapsed from the time he activated his lights until the vehicle came to a stop?

A. It was a relatively short amount of time. Probably within a block.

Q. How much time elapsed from the time you saw the Lexus go by, he made the statement that you concurred with, and you put on the emergency lights?

A. It happened very quickly. It was almost—the Lexus passed, he made the statement, and we initiated our lights.

Q. So from the time you made the observation until the stop, it would have been within a one block area?

A. A block to two blocks.

Q. But from the time you made your observation till the lights go on would have been less than a block, correct?

A. Yes.

Q. Because then after that there would have been reaction time and—did your vehicle get behind the other vehicle at the time you activated the lights, in other words, attempt to pursue it?

A. I believe so, yes.

Q. So you moved into the right-hand lane, and then he signaled to the left, and did you follow him back over?

A. I believe so. I'm not—I couldn't say for sure.

Q. OK. And, again, if you're not sure, that's an appropriate answer, too. I'm just trying to figure out what your recollection is, and I know it was some time ago. After you called in and then got out of the car, that would be pursuant to your training on a traffic stop, to take a position on the opposite side to observe any passengers in the vehicle, correct?

A. Sure. There's officer safety issues and what-not with any traffic stop.

Q. And when you did that, is that when you observed the woman in the passenger's side?

A.   Yes.

Q.   Then when you were satisfied there was no security issue with the woman and you heard the conversation on the other side, you moved then to the same side as your training officer?

A.   Correct.

Q.   Prior to you changing positions, did you hear anything that was being said by my client?

A.   I could not. I had traffic to my back that was going by.

Q.   So you didn't hear anything?

A.   No, I could not hear any conversation.

Q.   Did you make any observations about him at that point?

A.   Not from where I was. I couldn't get a good look at him.

Q.   When you then took your new position, which would be on the driver's side, what was the first thing you observed either hearing or visually?

A.   I observed Officer Conlee asking him for his operator's license and registration card.

Q.   Did he raise his voice?

A.   No.

Q.   Did you hear the woman crying, because Officer Conlee raised his voice?

A.   No.

Q.   What was the next thing you observed from your point of reference on the driver's side?

A.   Officer Conlee made several requests for the driver's license and registration card. The defendant, Mr. Stucky, was attempting to make a call on his cell phone.

Q. Did he have his credential case out at that point?

A. No.

Q. Did you ever see a credential case?

A. No.

Q. Did you see where the driver's license and registration that you observed came from?

A. I remember it was some sort of black case. Whether it was—you know, my recollection is it was some sort of day timer or—it didn't seem like a wallet.

Q. It didn't seem like a wallet?

A. No.

Q. But you couldn't see specifically from where you were?

A. No. I was positioned a little bit back so, no, I could not.

Q. Do you hear my client say anything at that point?

A. Not that I recall.

Q. And, again, there was no speed timing device utilized in this particular case, was there?

A. No.

MR. MANGES: Thank you. I have no further questions.

OFFICER CONLEE: I have a couple.

REDIRECT EXAMINATION

BY OFFICER CONLEE:

Q. Did you base you estimate of the speed of his vehicle on what I was saying, or was this your own opinion as far as how fast that vehicle was going?

A. You stated it was going by at a high rate of speed, approximately fifty to fifty-five miles per hour, and I agreed with that.

Q. But my question is did you agree with that because you felt that vehicle was going that speed or only because I was telling you that?

A. No, I agreed because I felt the vehicle was going that speed.

Q. When I activated my emergency lights, what lane was I in?

A. You were in the left lane.

Q. How soon after I activated my lights did the other vehicle move into the lane I was in and pull over to the curb?

A. It was a relatively short amount of time.

Q. Did I at any time move from the left lane over into the right lane, follow that vehicle, then back over into the left lane?

A. I don't remember for sure, no. I could not tell you.

Q. Did this gentleman, Clayton Stucky, ever at any time identify himself prior to the time I was issuing him the citations as a police officer or a member of the Nita State Police, whatever?

A. No.

Q. When we went back to write the citations, did you believe at that point—was there any reason for you to believe that he was a police officer?

A. No.

OFFICER CONLEE: Your Honor, I rest, and the City rests.

THE COURT: OK.

MR. MANGES: I have no recross as a result of that redirect.

THE COURT: You may step down.

MR. MANGES: We call Clayton Stucky to the stand.

CLAYTON STUCKY, called as a witness, being sworn, testified as follows:

DIRECT EXAMINATION

BY MR. MANGES:

Q. Sir, would you please state your full name for the record.

A. Clayton Stucky.

Q. And your occupation, sir?

A. Nita State Police Officer.

Q. How long have you been a trooper with the Nita State Police?

A. It will be ten years in January.

Q. Drawing your attention specifically to the date and time in question, did you have occasion to be in the 700 block of East Market Street in Nita City?

A. Yes, sir.

Q. Could you tell us where you were going and what you were doing?

A. I just finished running some errands and doing some shopping in the city. My girl-friend and I were on our way to lunch.

Q. What were you wearing?

A. I was dressed down. I was in urban gear: baggy sweatpants, baggy shirt, a New York Yankees hat flipped backwards.

Q. While you were traveling on East Market Street, did you have occasion to observe a marked police unit?

A. I did.

Q. Where was that?

A. We were at a light at Broad Street. It was a red light. I was in the right lane, and the Nita City police car was in the left lane. I happened to look over at the officers. I didn't make any—just seen them. I looked over, and that was that. Moments later, the light turned green. The police car proceeded first. After that, it appeared to me that he was slowing up, maybe looking for something, someone. At that point, I drive right by him. The minute I crossed his front bumper, the lights came on. He came behind me in the right lane, which was at Fulton Street. I'm thinking he wanted to get over. At that point, I proceeded back in the left lane. He followed me to the left lane. I knew at that point he wanted me to pull over, so I stopped in the left parking lane.

Q. Tell me what happened from the time then that you pulled over to the left side by the meter. What occurred then?

A. At that point, my girlfriend asked, why are we being pulled over? I said I'm not sure; I'm going to find out in a minute. The officer came up to my car to the driver's side. He asked for my operator's license and owner's card. I reached for my wallet and asked him why I was being pulled over. At that point, he got real loud, I want to see your license and owner's card, registration card.

I began to reach to where—I have a black bag for carrying my service revolver and my badge case, which houses my license. It was in behind my girlfriend's seat. I began to reach back for that, and I asked him again, why are you pulling me over? Well, that got him more agitated because he began yelling, I'm not going to tell you again, give me your license and owner's card. When he did that, then my girlfriend got upset, and she started to cry. So now my attention was diverted from my badge case and my black bag to my girlfriend. I just asked my girlfriend to calm down, it's going to be OK, just relax.

Then he asked again. As I've been trained, you know, I knew something was wrong here. I picked up the cell phone and pushed speed dial to my commanding officer. While doing that, I then reached in my glove box, and asked him again why are you pulling me over, no response. At some point I got my badge case out of my black bag behind the passenger's seat. I got my registration out of the glove box. I opened up my badge case, which houses my license underneath my ID. I opened it up, gave him my license and owner's card for the car.

Q. After you did that, did you feel that you were required to verbalize the fact that you were a member of the state police?

A. Well, we're trained not to—it's a violation to display your badge in attempt to get out of something. I felt I didn't do anything wrong, so there was no reason to verbalize who I was.

Q. OK. What happened then?

A. He proceeded to say you're going to get a citation now. I was a little bit confused. I said you're kidding. He said no, I'm not. I said OK, and he walked back to his car.

Q. Do you believe at any point you were traveling fifty miles an hour on that particular road?

A. It never happened, never.

CROSS-EXAMINATION

BY OFFICER CONLEE:

Q. Mr. Clayton Stucky, how long have you been a member of the state police?

A. It will be ten years in January.

Q. And what are your duties there?

A. Routine patrol, investigating accidents. Traffic enforcement is the primary mission out there.

Q. When I came up to your vehicle and I asked for your driver's license and your registration card, what was the first thing that you said?

A. Why are you pulling me over.

Q. And did I explain to you why I pulled you over?

A. No, you did not.

Q. I didn't explain that to you?

A. No, sir.

Q. How many times did I ask you for your driver's license and registration card before you actually presented it to me?

A. Two or three times.

Q. So if I would have said like five or six times, I wouldn't be correct?

A. That wouldn't be correct, no.

Q. Do you recall our conversation in its entirety?

A. No, I do not.

Q. Do you recall me saying to you just prior to issuing the citations are you a police officer?

A. I recall you saying that, yes.

Q. Do you recall what caused me to ask you that?

A. I have no idea what caused you to ask me that.

Q. Did you, in fact, say to me in your own words, don't you honor a brother?

A. No, I did not say that.

Q. You did not make that statement to me?

A. I never said that.

Q. And are you telling the Court that after I pulled out within a short period of time I was doing something and you just drove by me—at what speed? You never said how fast you were going. How fast were you going? What's the maximum speed you were driving?

A. Twenty-five, thirty.

Q. You were driving twenty-five to thirty miles an hour?

A. I was in no rush to go nowhere.

Q. So, basically, everything that I've testified to today I'm either falsifying or apparently must have had the wrong vehicle or there's some other reason?

A. That's your words, sir.

Q. That's my words. And nothing—and you're not—and you didn't come into court—and as you're sitting there and took an oath, you're not lying to the Court?

A. No, sir.

OFFICER CONLEE: Your Honor, I don't have any further questions.

THE COURT: Anything further?

REDIRECT EXAMINATION

BY MR. MANGES:

Q. Do any of the questions that were just asked change your testimony regarding how that incident occurred and how fast you were going?

A. No, sir.

Q. And, again, when the car pulled behind you in the right lane, that's when you moved into the left lane because you thought it was going after something else or—

A. I wasn't doing anything to cause the lights, so I assumed he was looking for someone or going somewhere. So as it got behind me, I got out of his way.

Q. That's why you got in the left lane?

A. Right.

Q. When he followed you back into the left lane, did you then conclude that—

A. I knew he wanted to pull me over.

Q. And that's why you pulled over in the left lane, correct?

A. Yes, sir.

Q. Would there have been parking on the right-hand side to pull over, if you were so inclined?

A. Yes, sir.

MR. MANGES: That would be the full extent of the defense as well. We rest.

THE COURT: OK. Any closing statements from the defense?

MR. MANGES: Yes, Your Honor, if I might.

(Mr. Manges closed to the Court on behalf of the defendant.)

(Officer Conlee closed to the Court on behalf of the City.)

THE COURT: I would like to start off by saying that given the fact that the defendant in this case is a trooper, the use of the profiling argument for the stop should be offensive to him and his job, as well as it is to this Court and, the Court takes some offense that that excuse was used for why this defendant was stopped.

Having said that, I do find reasonable doubt as to the defendant's speed. Given everyone's testimony, no one has stated that the defendant's car was out of control, no one has stated that he came anywhere near hitting anyone. I have reasonable doubt as to his speed because I have not been given anything that is beyond a reasonable doubt to show that he was in excess of the speed limit, so I will find him not guilty of the speed violation.

(The hearing was concluded at 11:45 a.m.)

I hereby certify that the proceedings and evidence are contained fully and accurately in the notes taken by me on the within proceedings and that this copy is a correct transcript of same.

/s/ *Patsy A. Sitwell*
Patsy A. Sitwell, Reporter
Notary Public

Exhibit 11

Clinton T. Manges
Attorney at Law

3964 Lexington Street

Nita City, Nita 09101

Phone: 322-555-6283

Facsimile: 322-555-2964

Email: CTMLaw@gmail.nita

November 15, YR-2

Re: Commonwealth v. Clayton Stucky

Initial meeting—10/14/YR-2 .... $250.00

Representation at Preliminary Hearing—11/5/YR-2 .... $1,000.00

TOTAL AMOUNT DUE............ $1,250.00

**************PAYABLE IN FULL IMMEDIATELY UPON RECEIPT******************

Exhibit 12

Nita Internal Medicine Associates

249 Landon Lane

Nita City, Nita 09102

322-555-6722

9 April YR-1

To whom it may concern:

Clayton Stucky is a patient at our practice who has been under my care. Please excuse him from work for medical concerns beginning 3/11/YR-1 to 4/11/YR-1. He may return to work 4/12/YR-1. Please call our office with any further questions.

Sincerely,

/s/ *Anna Stovall*
Anna Stovall, MD

Exhibit 13

**Collins & Associates
8 Wyntre Brooke Drive
Elmerton, Nita 09103**

July 26, YR-1

Re: Clayton Stucky

To whom it may concern:

Trooper Clayton Stucky continues to be under my professional care. Please excuse him from work duty as of this date. A return to work date is pending.

Sincerely,

/s/ *Leslie Collins*
Leslie Collins, PhD

**(332) 555-3827
collinsmedical.nita**

Exhibit 14

**Collins & Associates
8 Wyntre Brooke Drive
Elmerton, Nita 09103**

July 30, YR-1

Re: Clayton Stucky

To whom it may concern:

Trooper Clayton Stucky has been under my professional care. I am releasing him to return to full work duty as of Monday, 8/2/YR-1.

Sincerely,

/s/ Leslie Collins
Leslie Collins, PhD

**(332) 555-3827
collinsmedical.nita**

Exhibit 15

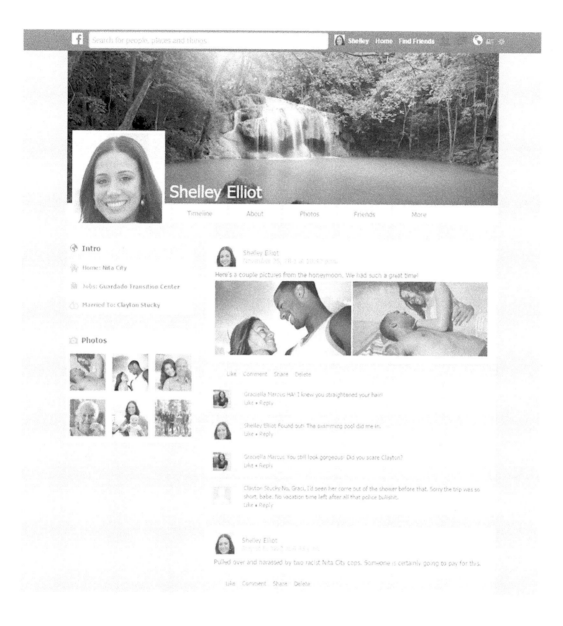

Shelley Elliot
October 20, Yr-2 at 6:14 p.m.

Grandma's birthday was so much fun. My baby sis came into town and surprised us all. Great picture of her with Dad. ¡Feliz cumpleaños abuelita!

Like   Comment   Share   Delete

Shelley Elliot
October 22, Yr-2 at 4:15 p.m.

I do not know how Clayton does what he does. Being a police officer of color is a thankless task. He has to tolerate bigotry from the white drivers he stops, and being called an "Uncle Tom" by those of color. Now I understand when he says he sees his job as another call to serve his country. God bless him.

Like   Comment   Share   Delete

Shelley Elliot
February 16, Yr-1 at 11:12 a.m.

Just got back from an incredibly frustrating meeting with the school principal. She did not seem to care that my daughters' classmates make disparaging comments about their race and ethnicity. I suppose we should not put all the blame on the kids, who are just repeating what they hear from their parents at home. Praying to God to keep my babies safe, and praying for the principal to get some education herself.

Like   Comment   Share   Delete

Shelley Elliot

I couldn't resist a picture with a client's baby. It's nice to see smiling faces at my office!

Like   Comment   Share   Delete

Graciela Marcus > Shelley Elliot

Here's the picture from our hike. I knew you and Clayton were gonna hit it off!

Like   Comment   Share   Delete

Shelley Elliot

I am beginning to understand why there were race riots in Nita City in the late 1960s. If ten percent of the complaints I see filed with the Human Relations Commission are true, there is a powerful segment of our community whose attitudes have not changed one bit!

Like   Comment   Share   Delete

There are no more posts to show.

Facebook © VR :   English (US)

Exhibit 16

Nita City
Police Department

Traffic Enforcement Training Manual

LAW ENFORCEMENT CODE OF ETHICS

AS A LAW ENFORCEMENT OFFICER, my fundamental duty is to serve mankind; to safeguard lives and property; to protect the innocent against deception, the weak against oppression or intimidation, and the peaceful against violence or disorder; and to respect the Constitutional rights of all men to liberty, equality, and justice.

I will keep my private life unsullied as an example to all; maintain courageous calm in the face of danger, scorn, or ridicule; develop self-restraint; and be constantly mindful of the welfare of others. Honest in thought and deed in both my personal and official life, I will be exemplary in obeying the laws of the land and the regulations of my department. Whatever I see or hear of a confidential nature or that is confided to me in my official capacity will be kept ever secret unless revelation is necessary in the performance of my duty.

I will never act officiously or permit personal feelings, prejudices, animosities or friendships to influence my decisions. With no compromise for crime and with relentless prosecution of criminals, I will enforce the law courteously and appropriately without fear or favor, malice or ill will, never employing unnecessary force or violence and never accepting gratuities.

I recognize the badge of my office as a symbol of public faith, and I accept it as a public trust to be held so long as I am true to the ethics of the police service. I will constantly strive to achieve these objectives and ideals, dedicating myself before God to my chosen profession . . . law enforcement.

NITA CITY POLICE DEPARTMENT (VEHICLE CODE)

I.   Policy

It shall be the policy of the Nita City Police Department that all officers who are qualified be trained in traffic enforcement.

II.   Procedure

Each designated police officer will receive a minimum of five (5) consecutive days of supervised traffic enforcement training. The traffic field-training officer will instruct the officer in specific areas of training that will include the following:

1.   General knowledge of the Nita Vehicle Code
2.   Safety in making traffic stops
3.   Identifying a violation of the Nita Vehicle Code
4.   Stopping a traffic violator and use of emergency equipment
5.   Approaching a traffic violator
6.   Explaining a traffic violation to the operator
7.   Completing a traffic citation
8.   Issuing a traffic citation
9.   Disposition of the traffic citation
10.   Hearings

Note: The traffic field-training officer will further instruct the officer on possible problems that might arise when dealing with a traffic violator.

III.   Evaluation

The traffic field-training officer will evaluate the officer using an officer traffic evaluation form. The evaluation shall begin at the start of traffic training and continue through the entire traffic field-training program. The traffic evaluation form is designed to measure the progress of the officer using a numerical score system. The traffic field-training officer will review the traffic evaluation form with the officer and request that the officer sign the evaluation form indicating he or she understood the evaluation. The traffic field-training officer will forward the copy of the traffic evaluation form to a traffic evaluation supervisor for review and retention. The officer in training must have a minimum acceptable evaluation to enforce traffic. An average rating of 3.0 shall be required.

TRAFFIC ENFORCEMENT TRAINING SCHEDULE

Five (5) Days, Forty (40) Hours

Day # 1:   Classroom Instruction

       a.   Nita Vehicle Code
       b.   Rules of Criminal Procedure
       c.   Traffic Stops
       d.   Traffic Citation
       e.   General Information

Day #2:   Traffic Stop Instruction

       a.   Observing Traffic
       b.   Observing Traffic Violations
       c.   Making Traffic Stops
       d.   Practice Prototype Citations
       e.   Questions and Answers

Day #3:   Traffic Stop Instruction

       a.   Observing Traffic
       b.   Observing Traffic Violations
       c.   Verbal Warnings by Officer in Training
       d.   Questions and Answers

Day #4:   Traffic Stops

       a.   Traffic Citations Issued by Officer in Training
       b.   Oral or Written Test
       c.   Questions and Answers
       d.   Evaluation

Day # 5:   Traffic Stops

       a.   Officer in Training
       b.   Oral or Written Test
       c.   Questions and Answers
       d.   Evaluation

Training Comments: _____

_____
_____
_____
_____
_____

Nita City Police Training (Traffic Stops)

The following guidelines involve the training of a police officer in stopping a subject for violating the Nita Vehicle Code. The training will include the actual stop, approaching the operator, issuing a traffic citation, and the disposition of the traffic citation. The training may involve a written test to determine what the officer has learned through his or her training. The officer will be evaluated on the training that is presented.

The following information will be covered during the training.

1.   General Knowledge of the Nita Vehicle Code

     a.   Chapter 13   Registration of Vehicles
     b.   Chapter 15   Licensing of Drivers
     c.   Chapter 31   General Provisions
     d.   Chapter 75   Rules of the Road in General
     e.   Chapters 41, 43, 45   Equipment Violations
     f.   Chapter 47   Inspection of Vehicles

2.   Safety. The officer will be instructed on making a traffic stop in a safe manner. The instructions will include the manner in which the violator is stopped after the traffic violation is observed, the proper position of the police vehicle at the location where the violator is stopped, and the use of the emergency equipment.

3.   Observing a violation of the Nita Vehicle Code. The officer will be instructed on how to identify certain violations such as general moving violations, inspection violations, and equipment violations.

4.   The Traffic Citation. The officer will be instructed on the proper way to complete a traffic citation. The officer will complete blank prototype citations prior to the actual issuing of a traffic citation. Special emphasis will be put on accuracy and neatness.

5.   Explaining the Traffic Citation. The officer will be instructed on the proper way to explain the violation to the operator, how to issue a traffic citation to the operator, and how to answer any questions that might come up during the traffic stop.

6.   Disposition of the Traffic Citation. The officer will be instructed on the proper way to dispose of the traffic citation, which will include where to place the officer's copy of the traffic citation and the copies that go to the municipal court.

7.   Problem Areas. The officer will be instructed on some problem areas that might arise during routine traffic stops. Some of the problem areas are as follows:

     a.   The operator appears to be intoxicated.
     b.   The operator is driving under suspension or is driving without a license.
     c.   Multiple violations such as vehicle not inspected, no insurance, misuse of a registration.
     d.   The operator refuses to identify himself or herself or gives false information.
     e.   The operator refuses to sign the citation or accept the citation.
     f.   The operator is wanted.

g.   Towing the vehicle.

h.   Selling the violation and avoiding arguments.

8.   Hearings. The officer will be instructed on what to do should the traffic violation result in a traffic hearing at the office of a district justice or in the court of common pleas. The officer will be instructed at a later time on how to testify in court.

TRAFFIC STOP

The single most important factor in any traffic stop is the safety of the officer. Safety starts when an officer observes a traffic violation. The officer should attempt to make the traffic stop using the following guidelines.

(1) When making a traffic stop always activate all emergency lights. The use of a siren device is an option that should be used when the violator fails to pull over in a reasonable time or it is apparent that the violator doesn't see the emergency lights.

(2) The actual stop of the violator should always be made at a safe location. An officer should attempt to stop the violator on the right berm or nearest to the right edge of the roadway or in a parking lot. Always attempt to stop the vehicle where you feel safe and not where the violator takes you. Note: The operator of the vehicle may be wanted and has no idea you are stopping him for a violation of the vehicle code.

(3) The officer should attempt to position his or her police vehicle about a vehicle length to the rear of the violator with the left front of the officer's vehicle extending out to the left a few feet to provide a safe area for the officer to stand while talking to the violator. Some officers like to angle their police vehicle slightly so they can have additional safety from traffic and from the violator should an incident occur. Note: Unless it is not an option, never stop a vehicle on the center of any roadway, on the crest of a hill, or anywhere else that isn't safe.

(4) Before approaching the violator, always advise Nita City Control that you have a traffic stop. You should include the location of the stop, the license plate number of the vehicle, and anything else that might be deemed suspicious. Always request a back-up unit if you feel the traffic stop is anything less than routine.

(5) An officer should always make sure he or she is clear to step out of the police vehicle. Other operators often take their attention off the roadway to observe the traffic stop, creating a danger to the officer exiting the patrol car. At night, some officers use their headlights or take-down lights for extra security. Not only does this provide increased visibility of the stopped vehicles for other drivers, the lights make it more difficult for the violator to observe the officer as he approaches the driver's door. The officer should keep close to the left side of the vehicle while approaching the driver's door, reducing the chance of being struck by another vehicle or being in full view of the operator. The officer may want to check the trunk as he passes by the vehicle to see if the trunk is open. Officers have on occasion discovered persons in the truck, either trapped by the car's passengers or hiding to avoid apprehension. The officer should be in a position where he or she can observe all of the persons in the vehicle while explaining the violation.

(6) Start the conversation politely. Say, "Sir/ma'am, may I see your operator's license, registration card, and insurance card." Then explain the reason for the stop: "Sir/ma'am, I stopped you for failing to stop for a red light at East King Street and Haines Road." If there is feedback from the operator, listen to what the person has to say before deciding what you are going

to do. Sometimes the operator may have a good reason for committing the violation. If you decide to cite the operator, explain that you will write up the citation in the patrol car and then return to his vehicle and explain the citation. Return to your vehicle and complete the citation. When you are finished writing the citation, proofread for errors. Some mistakes on a citation are grounds for dismissal. Note: Take your time. There is no reason to hurry. Decide whether to run a warrants check on the operator's license.

(7) When you return to the operator, again explain the violation and then explain how the citation can be handled: "Sir, you have ten days to either pay the fine or request a hearing. There are directions on the lower portion of the citation and on the back of the citation." Ask the operator if he or she wishes to sign the citation. Explain that signing is not an admission of guilt. After the citation is signed or not signed, tear out the defendant's copy and hand to the operator. Before you leave, ask if there are any additional questions. Some officers say "good day" and return to their vehicle.

At times an operator will become angry and, in some cases, combative when issued a traffic citation. Conversations with a person who has been stopped for a violation are like fingerprints. No two are alike. Most operators are agreeable, but there are some exceptions. A traffic stop stresses operators, and some react to that stress with anger. Try to keep your cool—remember that their reaction is not personal—and do your best to diffuse the situation. Try to remain calm because the person who you just cited may file a complaint against you, and in the event of a hearing, he or she may bring up the complaint and harm your testimony. If you feel that the operator may file a complaint or, at a hearing, accuse you of unprofessional behavior, write a description of the interchange on the remarks section of the citation to preserve a record of the encounter.

Exhibit 17

Nita Township Police Department
Performance Evaluation Rating
Corporal

Name: Eric L. Conlee	Rank: Corporal Badge #: 31	Date: 2/22/YR-4	

Assignment Area: Patrol Supervisor   Period Covered: YR-5

Scoring:			
	1.0, 1.5	Inadequate -	Seldom if ever displays this characteristic
	2.0	Weak -	Occasionally displays this characteristic
	2.5, 3.0, 3.5	Average -	Usually displays this characteristic
	4.0	Good -	Displays this characteristic more than the average
	4.5, 5.0	Outstanding -	Always displays this characteristic

<u>Lack of Prejudice</u>: Does he enforce the laws with impartiality? Does he address all citizens with the respect that they deserve? Can he work effectively with any other officer within the department?   **3.0**

Nita Township Police Department
Performance Evaluation Rating
Corporal

Name: Eric L. Conlee   Rank: Corporal Badge #: 31   Date: 2/17/YR-5

Assignment Area: Patrol Supervisor   Period Covered: YR-6

Scoring:	1.0, 1.5	Inadequate -	Seldom if ever displays this characteristic
	2.0	Weak -	Occasionally displays this characteristic
	2.5, 3.0, 3.5	Average -	Usually displays this characteristic
	4.0	Good -	Displays this characteristic more than the average
	4.5, 5.0	Outstanding -	Always displays this characteristic

Lack of Prejudice: Does he enforce the laws with impartiality? Does he address all citizens with the respect that they deserve? Can he work effectively with any other officer within the department?   **4.0**

Nita Township Police Department
Performance Evaluation Rating
Corporal

Name: Eric L. Conlee   **Rank:** Corporal **Badge #:** 31   **Date:** 3/17/YR-6

Assignment Area: Patrol Supervisor- Field   **Training Period Covered:** YR-7

Scoring:	1.0, 1.5	Inadequate -	Seldom if ever displays this characteristic
	2.0	Weak -	Occasionally displays this characteristic
	2.5, 3.0, 3.5	Average -	Usually displays this characteristic
	4.0	Good -	Displays this characteristic more than the average
	4.5, 5.0	Outstanding -	Always displays this characteristic

Lack of Prejudice: Does he enforce the laws with impartiality? Does he address all citizens with the respect that they deserve? Can he work effectively with any other officer within the department?   **4.0**

Nita Township Police Department
Performance Evaluation Rating
Corporal

Name: Eric L. Conlee   Rank: Corporal Badge #: 31   Date: 3/11/YR-7

Assignment Area: Traffic/Road Supervisor   Period Covered: YR-8

Scoring:	1.0, 1.5	Inadequate -	Seldom if ever displays this characteristic
	2.0	Weak -	Occasionally displays this characteristic
	2.5, 3.0, 3.5	Average -	Usually displays this characteristic
	4.0	Good -	Displays this characteristic more than the average
	4.5, 5.0	Outstanding -	Always displays this characteristic

<u>Lack of Prejudice</u>: Does he enforce the laws with impartiality? Does he address all citizens with the respect that they deserve? Can he work effectively with any other officer within the department?   **3.5**

Nita Township Police Department
Performance Evaluation Rating
Corporal

Name: Eric L. Conlee   Rank: Corporal Badge #: 31   Date: 4/6/YR-8

Assignment Area: Patrol Supervisor   Period Covered: Y-9

Scoring:	1.0, 1.5	Inadequate -	Seldom if ever displays this characteristic
	2.0	Weak -	Occasionally displays this characteristic
	2.5, 3.0, 3.5	Average -	Usually displays this characteristic
	4.0	Good -	Displays this characteristic more than the average
	4.5, 5.0	Outstanding -	Always displays this characteristic

<u>Lack of Prejudice</u>: Does he enforce the laws with impartiality? Does he address all citizens with the respect that they deserve? Can he work effectively with any other officer within the department?   **3.5**

Nita Township Police Department
Performance Evaluation Rating
Corporal

Name: Eric L. Conlee   Rank: Corporal Badge #: 31   Date: 3/22/YR-9

Assignment Area: Road Supervisor   Period Covered: YR-10

Scoring:	1.0, 1.5	Inadequate -	Seldom if ever displays this characteristic
	2.0	Weak -	Occasionally displays this characteristic
	2.5, 3.0, 3.5	Average -	Usually displays this characteristic
	4.0	Good -	Displays this characteristic more than the average
	4.5, 5.0	Outstanding -	Always displays this characteristic

<u>Lack of Prejudice</u>: Does he enforce the laws with impartiality? Does he address all citizens with the respect that they deserve? Can he work effectively with any other officer within the department?   **4.0**

Nita Township Police Department
Performance Evaluation Rating
Corporal

Name: Eric L. Conlee   Rank: Corporal Badge #: 31   Date: 3/4/YR-10

Assignment Area: Road Supervisor   Period Covered: YR-11

Scoring: 1.0, 1.5   Inadequate -   Seldom if ever displays this characteristic
            2.0   Weak -   Occasionally displays this characteristic
            2.5, 3.0, 3.5   Average -   Usually displays this characteristic
            4.0   Good -   Displays this characteristic more than the average
            4.5, 5.0   Outstanding -   Always displays this characteristic

<u>Lack of Prejudice</u>: Does he enforce the laws with impartiality? Does he address all citizens with the respect that they deserve? Can he work effectively with any other officer within the department?   **4.0**

Nita Township Police Department
Performance Evaluation Rating
Corporal

Name: Eric L. Conlee   Rank: Corporal Badge #: 31   Date: 2/25/YR-11

Assignment Area: Road Supervisor   Period Covered: YR-12

Scoring:
1.0, 1.5	Inadequate -	Seldom if ever displays this characteristic
2.0	Weak -	Occasionally displays this characteristic
2.5, 3.0, 3.5	Average -	Usually displays this characteristic
4.0	Good -	Displays this characteristic more than the average
4.5, 5.0	Outstanding -	Always displays this characteristic

<u>Lack of Prejudice</u>: Does he enforce the laws with impartiality? Does he address all citizens with the respect that they deserve? Can he work effectively with any other officer within the department?   **3.5**

Nita Township Police Department
Performance Evaluation Rating
Corporal

Name: Eric L. Conlee   Rank: Corporal Badge #: 31   Date: 3/6/YR-12

Assignment Area: Road Supervisor   Period Covered: YR-13

Scoring: 1.0, 1.5   Inadequate -   Seldom if ever displays this characteristic
              2.0   Weak -   Occasionally displays this characteristic
              2.5, 3.0, 3.5   Average -   Usually displays this characteristic
              4.0   Good -   Displays this characteristic more than the average
              4.5, 5.0   Outstanding -   Always displays this characteristic

All scores below 2 and above 4 must be documented on reverse side.

Lack of Prejudice: Does he enforce the laws with impartiality? Does he address all citizens with the respect that they deserve? Can he work effectively with any other officer within the department?   **3.5**

Nita Township Police Department
Performance Evaluation Rating
Corporal

Name: Eric L. Conlee   Rank: Corporal Badge #: 31   Date: 9/20/YR-14

Assignment Area: Road Supervisor   Period Covered: YR-14

Scoring:	1.0, 1.5	Inadequate -	Seldom if ever displays this characteristic
	2.0	Weak -	Occasionally displays this characteristic
	2.5, 3.0, 3.5	Average -	Usually displays this characteristic
	4.0	Good -	Displays this characteristic more than the average
	4.5, 5.0	Outstanding -	Always displays this characteristic

All scores below 2 and above 4 must be documented on reverse side.

<u>Lack of Prejudice</u>: Does he enforce the laws with impartiality? Does he address all citizens with the respect that they deserve? Can he work effectively with any other officer within the department?   **3.5**

Nita Township Police Department
Performance Evaluation Rating
Corporal

Name: Eric L. Conlee   Rank: Corporal Badge #: 31   Date: 7/19/YR-14

Assignment Area: Road Supervisor   Period Covered: 5 – 6 YR-14

Scoring:	1.0, 1.5	Inadequate -	Seldom if ever displays this characteristic
	2.0	Weak -	Occasionally displays this characteristic
	2.5, 3.0, 3.5	Average -	Usually displays this characteristic
	4.0	Good -	Displays this characteristic more than the average
	4.5, 5.0	Outstanding -	Always displays this characteristic

All scores below 2 and above 4 must be documented on reverse side.

<u>Lack of Prejudice</u>: Does he enforce the laws with impartiality? Does he address all citizens with the respect that they deserve? Can he work effectively with any other officer within the department?   **3.5**

Nita Township Police Department
Performance Evaluation Rating
Corporal

Name: Eric L. Conlee   Rank: Corporal Badge #: 31   Date: 3/15/YR-14

Assignment Area: Road Supervisor   Period Covered: 1 – 4 YR-14

Scoring:			
	1.0, 1.5	Inadequate -	Seldom if ever displays this characteristic
	2.0	Weak -	Occasionally displays this characteristic
	2.5, 3.0, 3.5	Average -	Usually displays this characteristic
	4.0	Good -	Displays this characteristic more than the average
	4.5, 5.0	Outstanding -	Always displays this characteristic

All scores below 2 and above 4 must be documented on reverse side.

<u>Lack of Prejudice</u>: Does he enforce the laws with impartiality? Does he address all citizens with the respect that they deserve? Can he work effectively with any other officer within the department?   **3.5**

Nita Township Police Department
Performance Evaluation Rating
Corporal

Name: Eric L. Conlee   Rank: Corporal Badge #: 31   Date: 1/11/YR-14

Assignment Area: Road Supervisor   Period Covered: 11 – 12 YR-15

Scoring: 1.0, 1.5   Inadequate -   Seldom if ever displays this characteristic
             2.0   Weak -   Occasionally displays this characteristic
             2.5, 3.0, 3.5   Average -   Usually displays this characteristic
             4.0   Good -   Displays this characteristic more than the average
             4.5, 5.0   Outstanding -   Always displays this characteristic

All scores below 2 and above 4 must be documented on reverse side.

<u>Lack of Prejudice</u>: Does he enforce the laws with impartiality? Does he address all citizens with the respect that they deserve? Can he work effectively with any other officer within the department?   **3.0**

Nita Township Police Department
Performance Evaluation Rating
Corporal

Name: Eric L. Conlee   Rank: Corporal Badge #: 31   Date: 11/10/YR-15

Assignment Area: Road Supervisor   Period Covered: 9 – 10 YR-15

Scoring:

1.0, 1.5	Inadequate -	Seldom if ever displays this characteristic
2.0	Weak -	Occasionally displays this characteristic
2.5, 3.0, 3.5	Average -	Usually displays this characteristic
4.0	Good -	Displays this characteristic more than the average
4.5, 5.0	Outstanding -	Always displays this characteristic

All scores below 2 and above 4 must be documented on reverse side.

<u>Lack of Prejudice</u>: Does he enforce the laws with impartiality? Does he address all citizens with the respect that they deserve? Can he work effectively with any other officer within the department?   **3.0**

Nita Township Police Department
Performance Evaluation Rating
Corporal

Name: Eric L. Conlee   Rank: Corporal Badge #: 31   Date: 3/17/YR-15

Assignment Area: Patrol   Period Covered: 1/1/YR-16 – 12/31/YR-16

Scoring: 1.0, 1.5   Inadequate -   Seldom if ever displays this characteristic
               2.0   Weak -   Occasionally displays this characteristic
               2.5, 3.0, 3.5   Average -   Usually displays this characteristic
               4.0   Good -   Displays this characteristic more than the average
               4.5, 5.0   Outstanding -   Always displays this characteristic

All scores below 2 and above 4 must be documented on reverse side.

Lack of Prejudice: Does he enforce the laws with impartiality? Does he address all citizens with the respect that they deserve? Can he work effectively with any other officer within the department?   **3.0**

Exhibit 18

Lance Parsell text message to Bethany Paget

●●●●○ AT&T LTE   12:39 PM   ⌁ ◉ ✳ ▬▭

❮ Messages (1) **bethany.paget** Details

Text Message
Aug. 5, Y⌗-2 12:38 PM

> Paget, any idea why the Chief wants to see me? Am I screwed? 😠

📷 Text Message   Send

Q W E R T Y U I O P
A S D F G H J K L
⬆ Z X C V B N M ⌫
123 😃 🎤   space   return

Exhibit 19

Bethany Paget text message to Lance Parsell

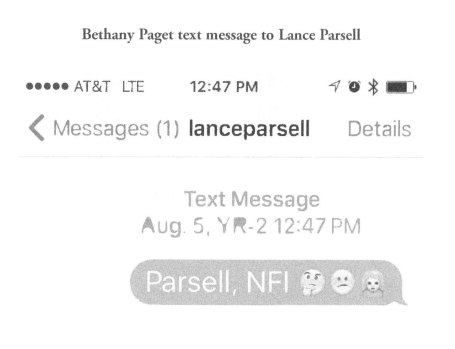

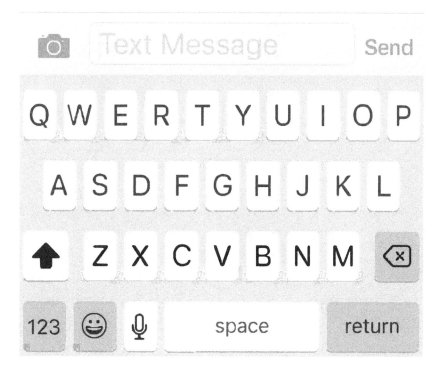

Exhibit 20

Nita City
Police Department

Rules, Policies,
and
Procedures Manual

POLICY MANUAL

INDEX

CHAPTER 1   GENERAL INFORMATION

CHAPTER 2   CODE OF CONDUCT

CHAPTER 3   GENERAL REQUIREMENTS

CHAPTER 4   DUTY REQUIREMENTS

CHAPTER 5   UNIFORM/EQUIPMENT

CHAPTER 6   DUTY PROVISIONS

CHAPTER 7   PRISONER TRANSPORT

CHAPTER 8   USE OF RESTRAINING DEVICES

CHAPTER 9   FIREARMS

CHAPTER 10   VEHICLE OPERATIONS

CHAPTER 11   C.L.E.A.N./N.C.I.C. TERMINAL OPERATIONS

CHAPTER 12   INFECTIOUS DISEASES

CHAPTER 13   HAZARDOUS MATERIALS

CHAPTER 14   DISCIPLINE

CHAPTER 15   PENALTY INDEX

CHAPTER 16   MANUAL INSPECTION

CHAPTER 17   CELL BLOCK POLICIES AND PROCEDURES

CHAPTER 1

GENERAL INFORMATION

Section 1.01   Distribution of Manual

Section 1.02   Additions or Revisions

Section 1.03   Definitions

SECTION ONE

GENERAL INFORMATION

The manual has been distributed to each police officer to equip him or her with a personal copy of those regulations that most directly affect his or her performance as a sworn officer of the Nita City Police Department. The manual's size and format is designed to provide an easy reference and a readily available source of information on procedures that pertain to an officer's role in a professional and progressive department.

1.01   DISTRIBUTION OF MANUAL

Each officer of the department shall be issued a manual, and such issuance shall be recorded on the officer's individual department property record.

1.02   ADDITIONS OR REVISIONS (Change Sheets)

Any changes in the Manual (whether a new or revised regulation) will be attached to a change sheet that will:

1.   Ensure total dissemination.
2.   Highlight the significant changes in procedure.
3.   Rescind conflicting regulations or directives.
4.   Provide instruction for proper insertion of the change into the manual.

1.03   DEFINITIONS

<u>Member</u>: Any full- or part-time Nita City Police Department Officer.

<u>Officer in Charge</u>: When two or more officers of the same rank are performing an assignment, a Superior Officer may designate an Officer in Charge (OIC).

<u>Superior Officer</u>: Any officer, holding the rank of Chief, Captain, Lieutenant, Sergeant, or Corporal.

CHAPTER 2

CODE OF CONDUCT

Section 2.01   Code of Ethics

Section 2.02   Oath of Office

Section 2.03   Conformance to Laws

SECTION 2

CODE OF CONDUCT

In order for the Nita City Police Department to be successful in meeting its responsibilities, it is vital to obtain the respect and confidence of the citizenry. Such desirable attitudes can be cultivated only by the efforts of each individual officer through his or her daily contact with the public. The principles set forth in this code of conduct are predicated upon the pronouncements found in the Law Enforcement Code of Ethics and Police Officer's Oath of Office.

2.01   CODE OF ETHICS

All officers of the Nita City Police Department shall obey the following code of ethics:

As a member of the Nita City Police Department, my first duty is to serve the people of Nita City.

I will safeguard lives and property, the weak against oppression or intimidation, and the peaceful against violence or disorder.

Above all else, I will respect the Constitutional rights of all men and women to liberty, equality, and justice.

I will keep my private life unsullied as an example to all; maintain courageous calm in the face of danger, scorn, or ridicule; develop self-restraint; and be constantly mindful of the welfare of others.

Honest in thought and deed in both my personal and official life, I will be exemplary in obeying the laws of the land and the regulations of my department.

Whatever I see or hear of a confidential nature or that is confided to me in my official capacity will be kept ever secret unless revelation is necessary in the performance of my duty.

I will never act officiously or permit my personal feelings, prejudices, animosities, or friendships to influence my decisions.

With no compromise for injustice and with relentless purpose of duty, I will enforce the law courteously and appropriately without fear or favor, malice or ill will, never employing unnecessary force or violence, and never accepting gratuities.

I recognize the badge of my office as a symbol of public faith, and I accept it, as a public trust to be held so long as I am true to the ethics of the Nita City Police Department.

I will constantly strive to achieve these objectives and ideals, dedicating myself before God to my chosen profession, Police Officer.

In order to abide by the Law Enforcement Code of Ethics and Police Officer's Oath of Office, each member of the department shall thoroughly familiarize himself or herself with and obey this code of conduct.

2.02 OATH OF OFFICE

I, (Your Name), appointed and commissioned by (Chief of Police's Name), Officer of the Police Department of Nita City, do solemnly swear that I will support, obey, and defend the Constitution of the United States and the Constitution of the State of Nita, and that I will discharge the duties of my office with fidelity: that I have not paid or contributed or promised to pay or contribute, either directly or indirectly, any money or other valuable thing to procure my appointment, and that I will not knowingly receive, directly or indirectly, moneys or other valuables for the performance or nonperformance of any act or duty pertaining to my office other than the compensation allowed by law.

Affirmed to and Subscribed

_____
(Your Name)
Police Officer

Before me this _____ day of _____, YR- ____

_____
(Chief's Name)
Chief of Police

2.03 CONFORMANCE TO LAWS

A police officer shall conform to and abide by the laws of the United States, the State of Nita, and all other states of the United States and subdivisions thereof.

CHAPTER 3

GENERAL REQUIREMENTS

Section 3.01   Unbecoming Conduct

Section 3.02   Loyalty to Department

Section 3.03   Dissemination of Information

Section 3.04   Seeking Publicity

Section 3.05   Badge of Office

Section 3.06   Display of Identification

Section 3.07   Associations

Section 3.08   Visiting Prohibited Establishments

Section 3.09   Joining Organizations

Section 3.10   Military Organizations

Section 3.11   Politics

Section 3.12   Use of Outside Influence

Section 3.13   Holding Office in Liquor Establishment

Section 3.14   Reporting Information

Section 3.15   Interference with Cases Assigned to Other Members

Section 3.16   Intervention in Arrest or Prosecution

Section 3.17   Interference with Discipline

Section 3.18   Alcohol and Substance Abuse Policy

Section 3.19   Testifying in Civil Cases

Section 3.20   Claims for Damages

Section 3.21   Bail

Section 3.22   Payment of Debts

Section 3.23   Internal Investigations

Section 3.24   Quarreling or Fighting with Officers

Section 3.25   Gambling

Section 3.26   False Enlistment

Section 3.27   Outside Employment

Section 3.28   Dissemination of News Releases

SECTION 3

GENERAL REQUIREMENTS

3.01 UNBECOMING CONDUCT

A member shall not conduct himself or herself in a manner that is unbecoming to a Police Officer. Unbecoming conduct is conduct that could reasonably be expected to destroy public respect for Police Officers and/or confidence in the Nita City Police Department.

3.02 LOYALTY TO DEPARTMENT

An officer shall not publicly criticize the Nita City Police Department, its policies, procedures, or other members or employees by talking, writing, or other expression, that is defamatory, obscene, or unlawful; or when the member knows that such criticism is false.

3.03 DISSEMINATION OF INFORMATION

An officer shall not disseminate, in any manner, any confidential information of the Nita City Police Department or its members, without proper authority. For the purposes of this regulation, confidential information shall be defined as that information that:

1.   a person could foresee that the disclosure thereof could:

    (a)   endanger an officer, or any other person;

    (b)   impede a just disposition of a case;

    (c)   aid a suspect to escape arrest;

    (d)   delay the apprehension of a criminal;

    (e)   permit the removal of stolen property or evidence by a suspect;

    (f)   compromise or negate the judicial process;

    (g)   violate a statute of the United States or the state of Nita pertaining to the release of designated confidential information;

    (h)   make known the contents of an internal or criminal investigation record or report to an unauthorized person.

2.   would identify a person who is acting as a confidential informant; except that an officer may divulge such identity to another officer when it is authorized by the proper authority and necessary in the performance of assigned duty.

3.04   SEEKING PUBLICITY

An officer shall not directly or indirectly seek publicity for himself or herself through the press, radio, television, or other news media, nor shall he or she furnish information to same for the purpose of gaining personal recognition as a Police Officer.

3.05   BADGE OF OFFICE

An officer shall not engage in any solicitation of individuals or businesses while in uniform or while using the badge of office. An officer shall not seek or accept any form of reward or compensation, excluding wages paid by the Nita City Police Department, as a result of his or her conduct while acting within the authority of his or her badge of office, except as directed by the Chief of Police. An officer shall not use or permit the use of his or her badge of office in any manner wherein it can reasonably be construed that the officer desires preferential treatment.

The term "badge of office" shall include the identification card, badge, official position, title, uniform, or any other tangible or intangible thing by which it can be construed that the concept of the Office of the Nita City Police Department is being interjected.

It is the specific intent of this section to limit the use of the member's badge of office to matters within the scope of his or her employment. This section shall not be construed to restrict any member in the free exercise of constitutionally protected freedoms that are not limited by the conditions of his or her employment.

3.06 DISPLAY OF IDENTIFICATION

Whenever an officer takes any lawful action, in the performance of his or her duty, he or she shall promptly and respectfully identify himself or herself by giving his or her rank and name, and other appropriate identification to persons involved. The officer in civilian clothes shall at all times carry his or her badge and official identification card, except when this is not feasible due to a specific duty assignment.

3.07 ASSOCIATIONS

An officer shall avoid associations or dealings with racketeers, known illegal gamblers, or persons who have a reputation in the community for criminal behavior, except in the performance of duty as directed by a superior. An officer, after being advised by a superior officer to avoid further associations or dealings with such individuals, shall be subject to disciplinary action if such associations or dealings continue.

3.08 VISITING PROHIBITED ESTABLISHMENTS

Frequenting, visiting, or entering a house of moral turpitude, gambling house, or establishment wherein any criminal law of the United States, the State of Nita, or any other state is violated shall be permitted only in the performance of duty as directed by superiors.

3.09 JOINING ORGANIZATIONS

An officer shall not, with the specific intent to further its aims, join or be a member of any organization or society that has as its purpose the overthrow of, or interference with, any lawfully constituted government of the United States, except in the performance of duty and while acting under proper and specific orders from a superior officer.

Exhibit 21

Nita City
Police Department

Training Division

Traffic Study – 1/1/YR-3 through 06/30/YR+1

YR-3 Census Report:
Nita County

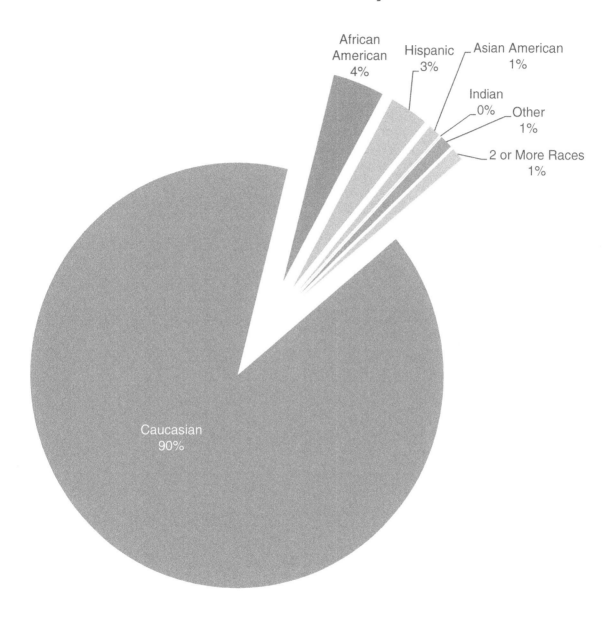

YR-3 Census Report: Nita City

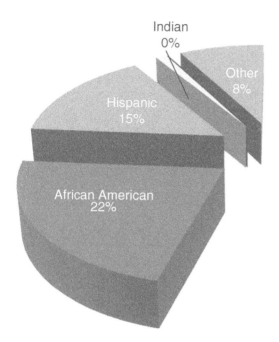
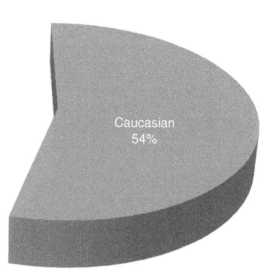

Indian
0%

Other
8%

Hispanic
15%

African American
22%

Caucasian
54%

YR-3 Traffic Stops

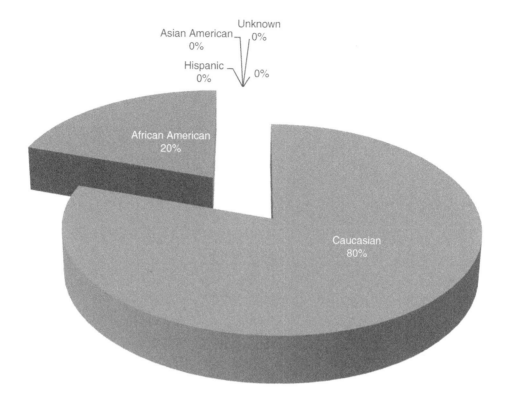

YR-2 Traffic Stops

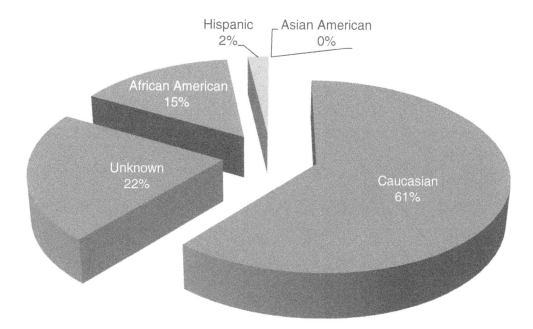

YR-1 Traffic Stops

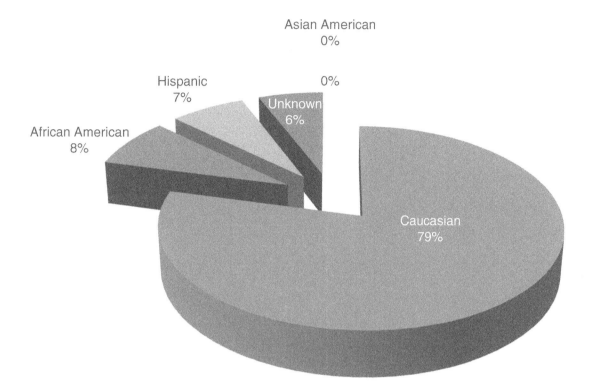

YR-0 Traffic Stops

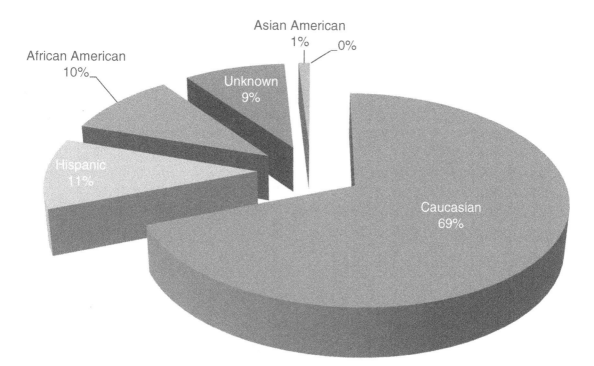

YR+1 Traffic Stops
as of 6/30/YR+1

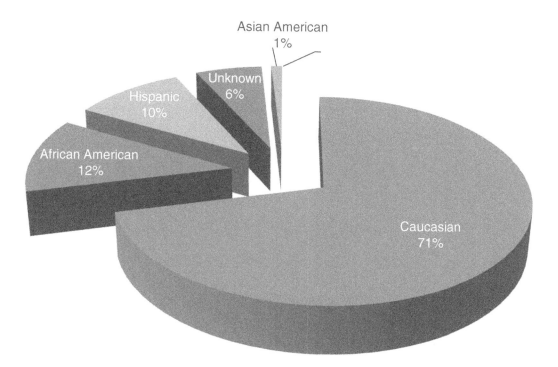

Nita City Police Department
Total Traffic Stops
01/01/YR-3 through 6/30/YR+1

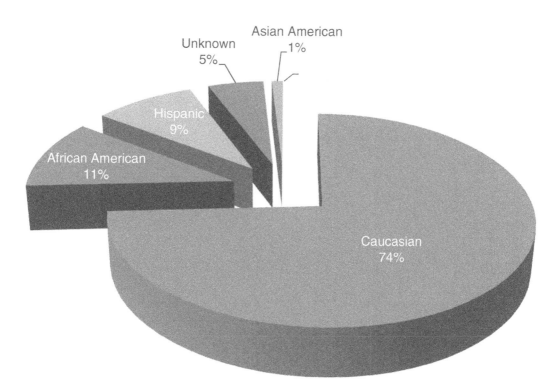

Officer Conlee
Total Traffic Stops as a
Nita City Police Officer

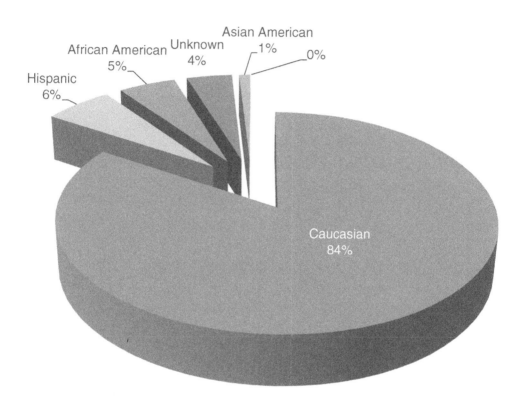

Officer Parsell
Total Traffic Stops as a
Nita City Police Officer

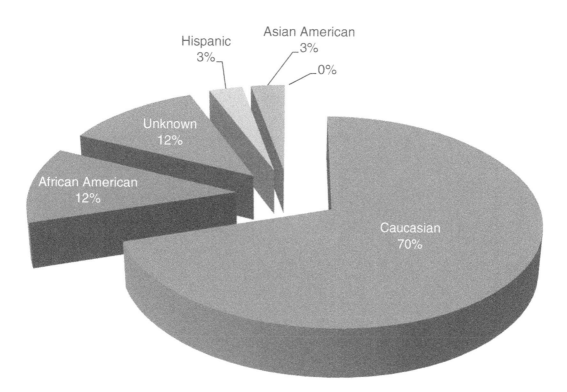

Exhibit 22

Nita
Gazette

© Nita Gazette   Tuesday, May 4, YR-1 $2.25

Racial profiling suit filed

A state trooper has filed a federal lawsuit against two Nita City Police Officers alleging that they stopped him because he was "driving while black."

Trooper Clayton Stucky alleges the traffic stop was a violation of his constitutional right to be safe from an unreasonable search and seizure and his right to equal protection. The suit also claims that Nita City is liable because its Chief of Police, Kurt Lieber, was deliberately indifferent in training and supervising city police officers as to the risk of racial profiling.

Nita City Chief of Police Lieber denied the claim and said Stucky was stopped on East Market Street because he was driving too fast for the rainy conditions at the time. "The charges are bulls ***. I'm sick of hearing about all this racial profiling crap," Lieber said.

Stucky's suit asks for unspecified compensatory and punitive damages and attorney's fees. It seeks damages for humiliation, pain and suffering, emotional distress, lost wages and medical bills.

Exhibit 23

TRUWEATHER

385 Science Park Road, State College, Nita 09106 800-555-0309
fax: 800-555-1339

The World's Weather Authority™   *email: info@truwx.nita www.truweather.nita*

July 16, YR-1

Mr. Ben Graham
American Civil Liberties Union
105 North Front Street, Suite 225
Nita City, Nita 99101

          Re: TruWeather File Number: 070420

Dear Mr. Graham:

Enclosed is a table that displays the hourly surface weather observation at Nita County Airport from 3:00 AM[1] to 3:00 PM on August 5, YR-2. At the airport, light rain fell from 10:27 AM until 11:40 AM. During that period, only 0.01 of an inch of rain was measured at the airport.

Thank you for choosing TruWeather as your source for weather information. We hope this information is useful to you. If you should have any additional questions or need additional information, please do not hesitate to contact us via email at forensic@truwx.nita or phone at (814) 555-8626.

                    Sincerely,

                    Ryan Grant
                    Manager of Forensic Services

RG:amb

---

1 All times are expressed in Eastern Daylight Time (EDT).

File: 07042—Official Weather Observations from Nita County Airport, Nita

for August 5, YR-2

Time[1]	General Weather	Visibility (Miles)[2]	Temperature (°F)	Wind Direction[3]	Wind Speed (MPH)	Rainfall during past hour (inches)
3:00 a.m.	Clear/Fog	2 ½	67	—	Calm	0
4:00 a.m.	Cloudy/Fog	2 ½	68	—	Calm	0
5:00 a.m.	Cloudy/Fog	3	70	—	Calm	0
6:00 a.m.	Cloudy/Fog	2 ½	72	—	Calm	0
7:00 a.m.	Cloudy/Fog	2	73	—	Calm	0
8:00 a.m.	Clear/Fog	2	74	—	Calm	0
9:00 a.m.	Mostly Clear/Fog	2 ½	75	—	Calm	0
10:00 a.m.	Rain/Fog	2	75	Southwest	3	0
11:00 a.m.	Mostly Clear	4	76	West	5	Trace[4]
12:00:00 Noon	Mostly Cloudy	5	77	West	7	0
1:00 p.m.	Partly Cloudy	7	77	Southwest	3	0
2:00 p.m.	Clear	10	79	—	Calm	0
3:00 p.m.	Clear	10	81	West	3	0

©TruWeather YR-1

---

1 All time references are express in Eastern Daylight Time (EDT).
2 The visibility at night is based on the ability to see a point source of light.
3 Indicates the direction from which the wind was blowing.
4 Trace is an amount too small to be measured. For rain it is less than 0.01 of an inch.

FINAL JURY INSTRUCTIONS

Plaintiff Clayton Stucky has filed three separate claims. You must decide each claim individually. I will now instruct you on each of these claims.

Stucky's first claim is that he suffered a violation of his right to be free from an unreasonable seizure under the Fourth Amendment to the United States Constitution, when defendants Conlee and Parsell allegedly effected the traffic stop without probable cause to believe that Stucky had committed a violation of the Nita City Vehicle Code. It is undisputed that the traffic stop constitutes a seizure under the Fourth Amendment. Therefore, in order to recover on this claim, Stucky must prove that Conlee and/or Parsell did not have probable cause to make the traffic stop.

Probable cause exists where the facts and circumstances known to the officer at the time of the seizure, in light of his law enforcement experience, are sufficient to warrant a person of reasonable prudence to believe that Stucky had committed a criminal offense. The only facts relevant in determining whether Conlee and Parsell had probable cause are those facts that were known to the officers at the time that the seizure occurred. Probable cause is an objective standard and must be measured according to a reasonable officer in the officers' position. Probable cause does not depend on the officers' own subjective beliefs. In other words, you may find probable cause existed to believe that Stucky had committed a particular offense even if Conlee or Parsell did not believe so or did not charge Stucky with that offense.

There are two criminal offenses under the Nita Vehicle Code that you may consider for purposes of determining whether probable cause existed. The first offense is driving a vehicle at an unsafe speed under Section 3361 of the Motor Vehicle Code. The second offense is driving a vehicle in excess of the maximum speed limit under Section 3362 of the Motor Vehicle Code. I will now explain the elements of each offense.

An individual may be found to have violated Section 3361 if he was driving at a speed greater than is reasonable and prudent under the conditions, and having regard to the actual and potential hazards then existing. Driving in excess of the speed limit does not by itself constitute a violation of Section 3361. Rather, there must be proof that the rate of speed at which the vehicle was driving was unreasonable under the then-existing circumstances. These circumstances include the amount of traffic, pedestrian travel, weather, visibility, nature of the roadway, presence of intersections, and any other factors bearing on the conditions. A speed is unreasonable if an ordinary motorist would not be able to maintain adequate control of his vehicle so as to avoid potentially subjecting other people and property to injury.

An individual may be found to have violated Section 3362 if he was driving at a speed in excess of the posted speed limit. The parties agree that the posted maximum speed limit in the area in which Stucky was driving was twenty-five miles per hour.

The Nita Motor Vehicle Code requires that to stop a motorist for driving in excess of the maximum speed limit, an officer must use a speedometer that was tested and calibrated for accuracy within sixty days of the stop and must follow a vehicle for three-tenths of a mile in order to obtain a valid estimate of speed. The Nita Supreme Court has ruled that an officer similarly must use a calibrated speedometer and must follow a vehicle for three-tenths of a mile in order to obtain a valid estimate of speed under Section 3361. These requirements of state law are one of the circumstances you may consider in determining whether Conlee and Parsell had probable cause.

Plaintiff Stucky's second claim is that he suffered a violation of his right to equal protection of the law under the Fourteenth Amendment of the United States Constitution. In order to recover on this claim, Stucky must prove that Conlee and/or Parsell were motivated by Stucky's race in making the traffic stop. You may consider Conlee's and Parsell's subjective beliefs as to the grounds for the stop, including the defendants' understanding of the requirements of Nita law that an officer must follow a vehicle for three-tenths of a mile and must use a calibrated speedometer in order to obtain a valid estimate of speed. Motivation may be established by statements or conduct of Conlee and Parsell, whether they occurred before, during, or after the traffic stop. You heard during the course of the trial certain evidence of prior matters involving Conlee and individuals of minority races. You may consider this evidence as potential proof of discriminatory intent. However, you must not consider such evidence as proof that Conlee has a bad character or has a propensity for taking certain actions. The fact that you may consider this evidence as an indication of Conlee's intent does not mean that you are obligated to accept the evidence as proof of intent.

In order to recover against either defendant Conlee or Parsell, plaintiff Stucky also must prove that the defendant caused the constitutional violation. A person is considered to have caused an act if his conduct played a substantial role in bringing about that act. It is insufficient to show mere acquiescence or knowledge of the act. The official must have somehow actively participated in the act through his conduct. This conduct may consist of physical actions that directly result in the happening of an act, or a verbal agreement and understanding that facilitates or encourages the happening of the act. Two persons may be found to have caused the same act if each of them substantially contributed to the happening of the act through his conduct.

Plaintiff Stucky's third claim is that Nita City is responsible for the violation of his constitutional rights because of the actions and inaction of Chief Lieber. More specifically, plaintiff Stucky alleges that Chief Lieber failed to properly train and supervise Nita City police officers as to the risk of racial profiling and that this failure to train and supervise was a cause of the actions of Conlee and Parsell in stopping Stucky based upon Stucky's race.

In order to find in favor of Stucky on this claim, you must have determined that Conlee and/or Parsell was motivated by Stucky's race in making the traffic stop. Stucky also must prove that Chief Lieber was deliberately indifferent to the risk of racial profiling in his training and supervision of Nita City Police officers. Specifically, Stucky must prove that in light of the duties assigned to Nita City police officers, the need for more or different training or supervision regarding the risk of racial profiling is so obvious, and the inadequacy so likely to result in the violation of constitutional rights that Chief Lieber can reasonably be said to have been deliberately indifferent to the need. Stucky must also prove that the deficiency in training or supervision actually caused Conlee and/or Parsell to use Stucky's race in making the traffic stop.

If you find in favor of plaintiff Stucky on any of his claims, you should award him all damages that he proves were caused by the violation of his constitutional rights. You may compensate Stucky for the following losses:

1. All legal expenses reasonably incurred for the defense of the traffic charges;

2. All medical expenses reasonably incurred for the diagnosis, treatment, and cure of injuries caused by the violation;

3. Any loss of earnings between the time of the traffic stop and the date of trial, as well as any loss or reduction of future earning capacity;

4. Physical or mental pain and suffering, embarrassment, humiliation, or loss of the ability to enjoy the pleasures of life; and

5. The value of the constitutional rights violated to Stucky.

If you find that defendant Conlee or Parsell acted in reckless disregard of plaintiff Stucky's constitutional rights, you also may award plaintiff Stucky punitive damages. The purpose of punitive damages is to punish the defendant and to deter others from violating the Constitution. However, you may not award punitive damages against Nita City.

UNITED STATES DISTRICT COURT
MIDDLE DISTRICT OF NITA

Clayton Stucky,   )
)
    Plaintiff,   )
)
v.   )   Civil Action No. CV-7620
)
Eric Conlee and Lance Parsell   )
in their individual capacities,   )
and Nita City, Nita,   )   JURY TRIAL DEMANDED
)
    Defendants.   )

FINAL VERDICT FORM

A.   **Claim for Unreasonable Seizure**

    1.   Do you find that defendant Conlee is liable for violating plaintiff Stucky's constitutional right to be free from an unreasonable seizure?

        Yes _____   No _____

    2.   Do you find that defendant Parsell is liable for violating plaintiff Stucky's constitutional right to be free from an unreasonable seizure?

        Yes _____   No _____

B.   **Claim for Equal Protection**

    3.   Do you find that defendant Conlee is liable for violating plaintiff Stucky's constitutional right to the equal protection of the law?

        Yes _____   No _____

    4.   Do you find that defendant Parsell is liable for violating plaintiff Stucky's constitutional right to the equal protection of the law?

        Yes _____   No _____

If you answered "No" to Question 3 and Question 4, do not answer Question 5. If you answered "Yes" to either Question 3 or Question 4, answer Question 5.

C. **Claim for Deliberate Indifference**

    5.   Do you find Nita City is liable because Chief Lieber was deliberately indifferent in training or supervising Nita City police officers as to the risk of racial profiling?

        Yes _____ No _____

D. **Damages**

    1.   State the amount of compensatory damages you award to Clayton Stucky

        $_____

    2.   State the amount of punitive damages you award to Clayton Stucky

        a. Punitive damages against Eric Conlee

        $_____

        b. Punitive damages against Lance Parsell

        $_____

                        _____

                        Jury Foreperson

CPSIA information can be obtained
at www.ICGtesting.com
Printed in the USA
BVHW011810140119
537774BV00017B/640/P